©Copyright 2024 - All rights reserved.

The content contained within this book may not be reproduced, duplicated, or transmitted without direct written permission from the author or the publisher.

Under no circumstances will any blame or legal responsibility be held against the publisher or author for any damages, reparation, or monetary loss due to the information contained within this book, either directly or indirectly.

Legal Notice:

This book is copyright-protected. It is only for personal use. You cannot amend, distribute, sell, use, quote, or paraphrase any part of the content within this book without the consent of the author or publisher.

Disclaimer Notice:

Please note the information contained within this document is for educational and entertainment purposes only. Every effort has been executed to present accurate, up-to-date, reliable, and complete information. No warranties of any kind are declared or implied. Readers acknowledge that the author is not engaged in rendering legal, financial, medical, or professional advice. The content within this book has been derived from various sources. Please consult a licensed professional before attempting any techniques outlined in this book.

By reading this document, the reader agrees that under no circumstances is the author responsible for any losses, direct or indirect, that are incurred as a result of the use of the information contained within this document, including, but not limited to, errors, omissions, or inaccuracies.

Table of Contents

Introduction 5
The Basics 7
How to Sit and Place Your Hands 7
The Keyboard: White Keys and Black Keys 9
Notes and Rests 12
Counting Beats 13
Music Sheets, Staffs, and Clefs 14

Chapter 1 — 17

Jolly Old St. Nicholas 18
Jesus, Joy of Man's Desiring 24
I Saw Three Ships 30

Chapter 2 — 35

Bring a Torch, Jeanette Isabella 36
We Wish You a Merry Christmas 42
We Three Kings of Orient Are 46

Chapter 3 — 53

Coventry Carol 54
The First Noel 60
God Rest You Merry, Gentlemen 66
Deck the Halls 72
Angels We Have Heard on High 76
Away In a Manger 82
Silent Night 86
O Come, O Come, Emmanuel 90

Chapter 4 — 95
O Little Town of Bethlehem — 96
Once in Royal David's City — 102
Hark, the Herald Angels Sing — 106
Auld Lang Syne — 112
Jingle Bells — 116
O Christmas Tree — 122
O Come All Ye Faithful — 128

Chapter 5 — 133
Here We Come A-Wassailing — 134
The Twelve Days of Christmas — 140
Happy Christmas — 148
Go Tell It on the Mountain — 154
It Came Upon the Midnight Clear — 162
Joy to the World — 168
What Child Is This — 174
Oh, Holy Night — 178
Conclusion — 183

Introduction

Hi, I'm Tempo the Turtle!

Hello, Piano Stars! Tempo the Turtle here, and I'm absolutely delighted to invite you to a jolly new piano adventure with our special collection of Christmas-themed songs just for you!

In this book, you'll find a wonderful selection of holiday tunes especially curated for young pianists. We will start with some easy and merry songs to help you get familiar with your piano keys. As you become more comfortable and confident, I will gradually introduce you to slightly more challenging pieces that will add extra sparkle to your seasonal celebrations. But don't worry - I'll be right here with tips and friendly guidance to make every practice session as enjoyable as a holiday treat.

Remember, learning piano is a journey: take your time, practice, have fun, and know that every practice session brings you closer to creating beautiful holiday music!

Are you ready to dive into the magic of Christmas music? Let's create some beautiful melodies together, one note at a time. I'm here to support you every step of the way, so let's get started and make this season truly musical and memorable!

The Basics
How to Sit and Place Your Hands

How you sit is very important when playing piano! If you want to sit and hold your hands correctly when playing piano, this is what you need to remember:

Sit up tall - don't slouch!

Keep your elbows at your sides without touching your body. They should make right angles so you aren't too close to the piano.

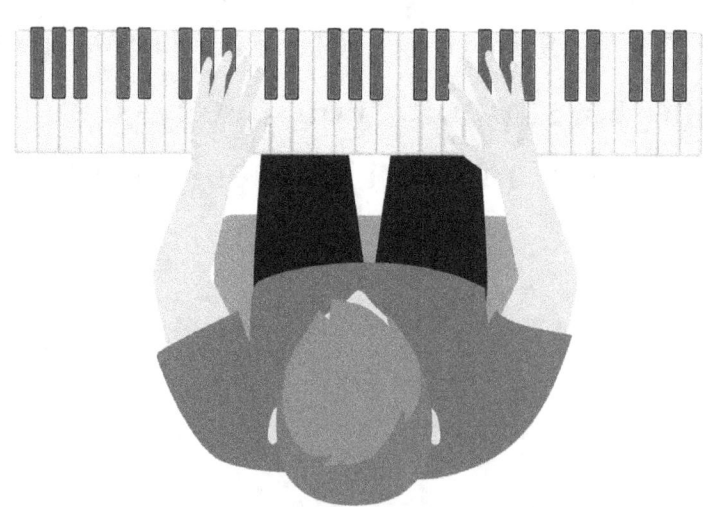

Sit towards the edge of the bench, and rest your feet on the floor or on a stool if your feet don't touch the floor.

Make sure that the bench is the right height, your feet should be touching the floor and your forearms should be parallel to the floor, too. You can sit on a cushion or a big book if you need to be a little taller.

Don't sit too close or too far from the keyboard. Your knuckles should touch the fallboard, or back of the piano, when you straighten your arm.

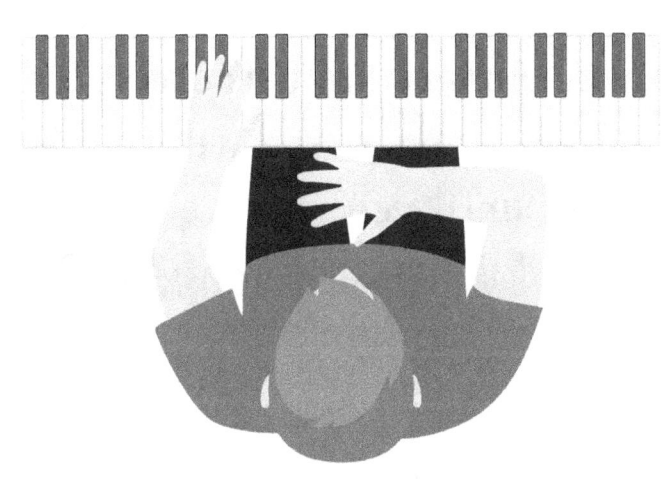

Keep your fingers curved, and use only the tips to play.

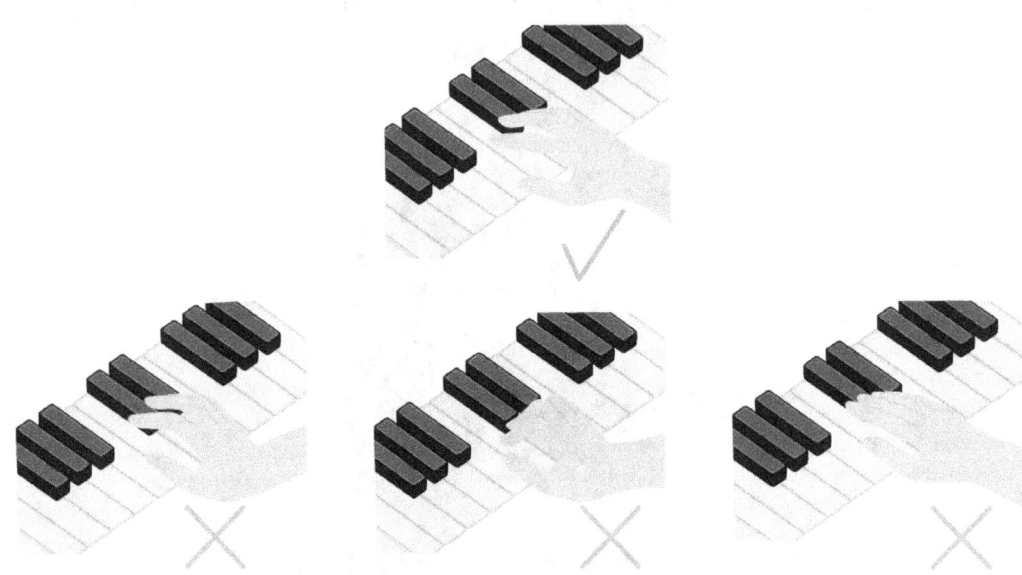

The Keyboard:
White Keys and Black Keys

The white keys are different music notes. They're named after the first seven letters of the alphabet, in this order: C, D, E, F, G, A, and B. When you reach note B, the next key will be C again, then D, and so on, with all the notes until you reach the end of the keyboard. Each key on the keyboard is half a step higher or lower than the key next to it.

You can also see black keys in groups of two and three. The black keys are just half a step higher or lower than the white keys they are next to, just like when two white keys are next to each other. These black keys are marked as sharps or flats.

A flat is half a step lower than the white key above it. A sharp is a half a step higher than the white key below it.

The most important key is the middle C. It's the C near the middle of the keyboard, to the left of a group of two black keys. Sometimes, it's not exactly in the middle of the keyboard. Sometimes, middle C is a little to the left. That's because some keyboards have more keys than others. You can see it right here:

49-Key Keyboard:

61-Key Keyboard:

76-Key Keyboard:

88-Key Keyboard:

Once you find middle C, you can use it to find all the other notes!

Learning key names and finger numbers can take some time. Here are two tips to make it easier:

1) Put a sticker on each key with its key name.

2) Write the number on your fingers with a washable marker!

Notes and Rests

Notes are special symbols that tell us what sounds to play on the piano and for how long:

Whole - 4 beats notes

Half notes - 2 beats

Quarter notes - 1 beat

Eight notes - Half a beat

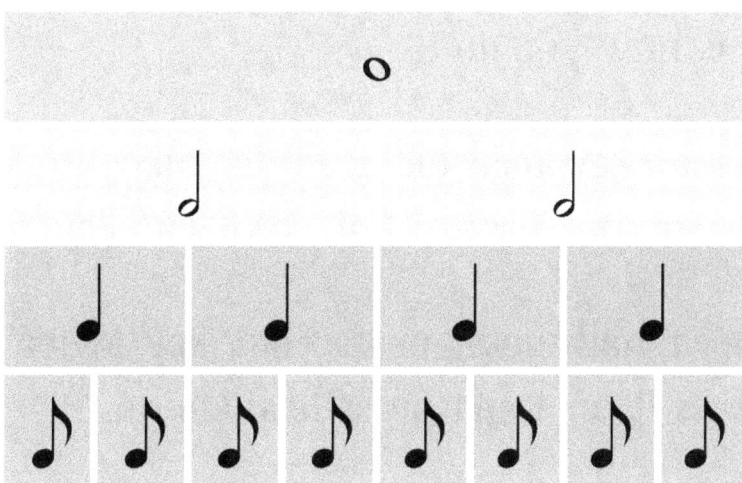

And rests are symbols that tell us when to take a break while playing the piano and for how long:

Whole rests - 4 beats

Half rests - 2 beats

Quarter rests - 1 beat

Eight rests - Half a beat

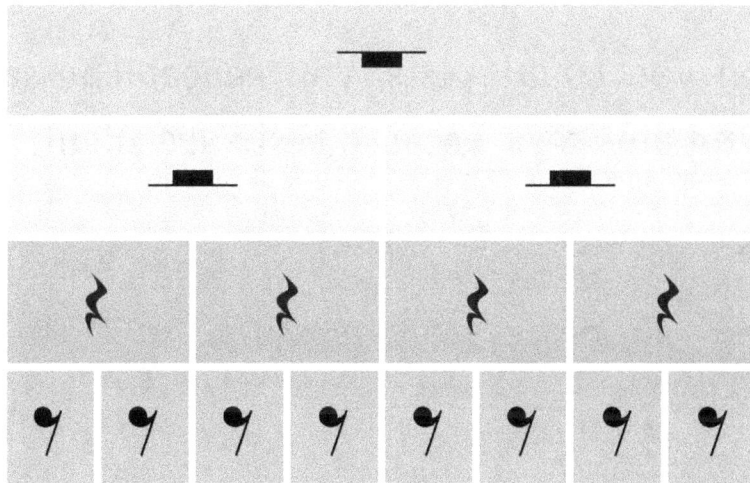

Counting Beats

There are many different ways to count beats. Counting numbers, clapping, tapping on the floor. Let's keep it simple and count beats out loud until you get used to it. Then you can count in your head. This is how you do it:

- Press a key and hold it while you count 1-2-3-4 evenly and slowly. When you reach 4, let go of the key, and- that's a whole note!

- For a half note, press that key twice while counting 1-2-3-4. Press it on 1 and press it again on 3.

- Then, press it four times while counting 1-2-3-4. Once for each number, that's a quarter note!

- Last but not least: the shortest note of all! Press the key twice for each number to see how fast an eighth note is: 1-and-2-and-3-and-4-and.

When you count rests, you repeat the same process but without playing any keys, because rests are silent!

Music Sheets, Staffs, and Clefs

You will be seeing a lot of these in this book! Music sheets are full of lines, notes, and fancy symbols. Those lines come in groups of five called a staff. Those staffs are the home of music notes. Each note lives on a different floor:

Notes for the treble clef and bass clef

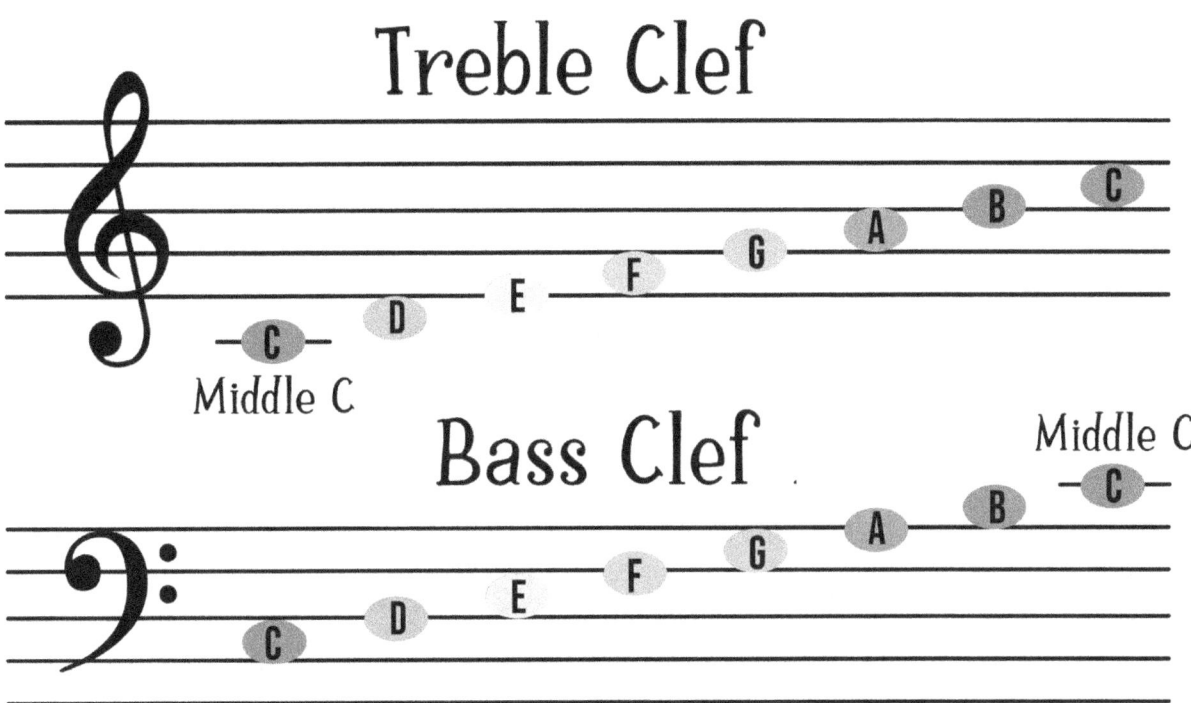

The most important fancy symbols are the clefs:

The treble clef tells you to play the higher notes on the right side of the keyboard. You usually play them with your right hand.

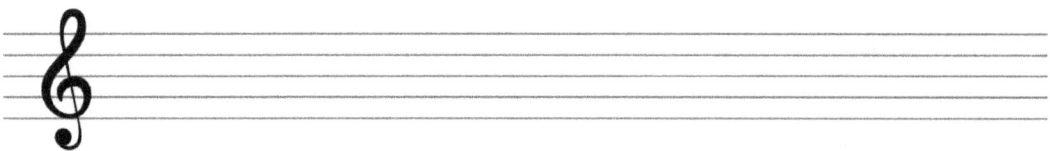

The bass clef tells you to play the lower notes on the left side of the keyboard. You usually play them with your left hand. Although this is useful information, you will not play in the bass clef in this book.

Next to the treble clef and the bass clef you will see two numbers stacked on top of each other. This is called the time signature. The number above tells you how many beats (counts) there are in each measure. The number below tells you what kind of beats they are. For example, if you see a number 6 above and a number 8 below, it means you count six beats in each measure and each beat has the value of an eighth note.

count to 6

Chapter 1

Jolly Old St. Nicholas

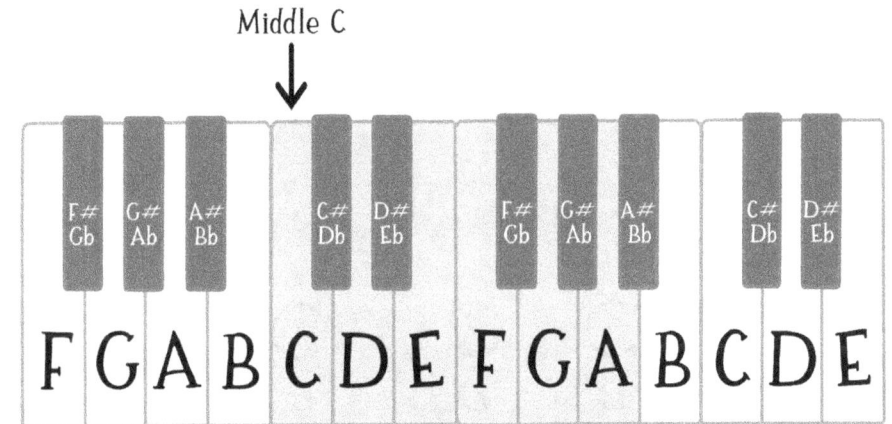

JOLLY OLD SAINT NICHOLAS

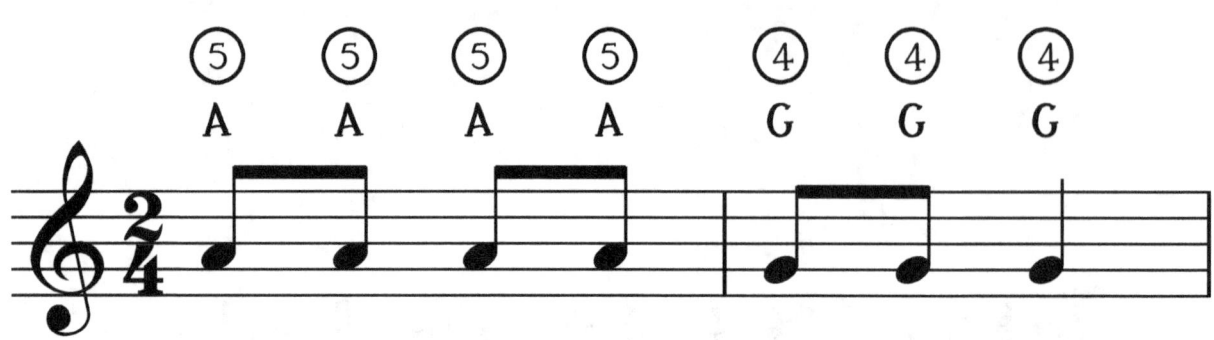

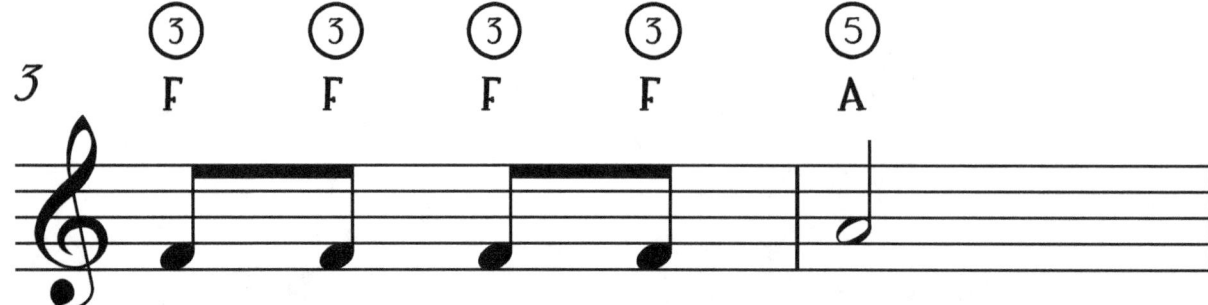

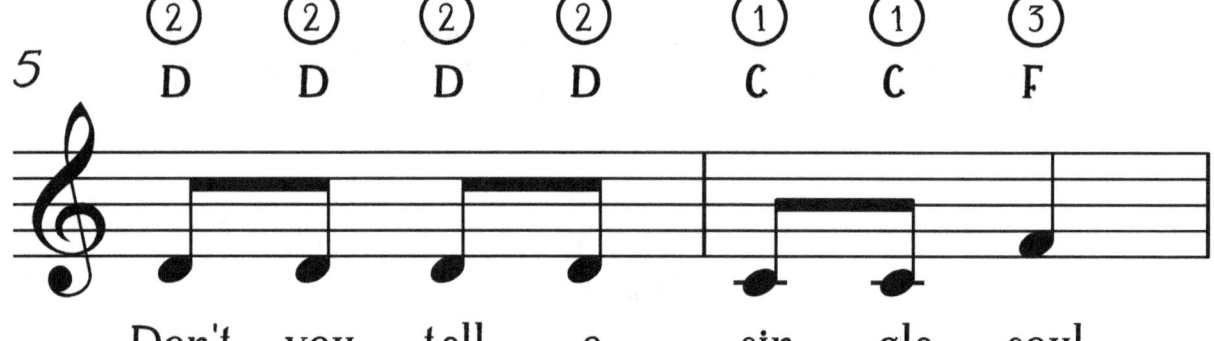

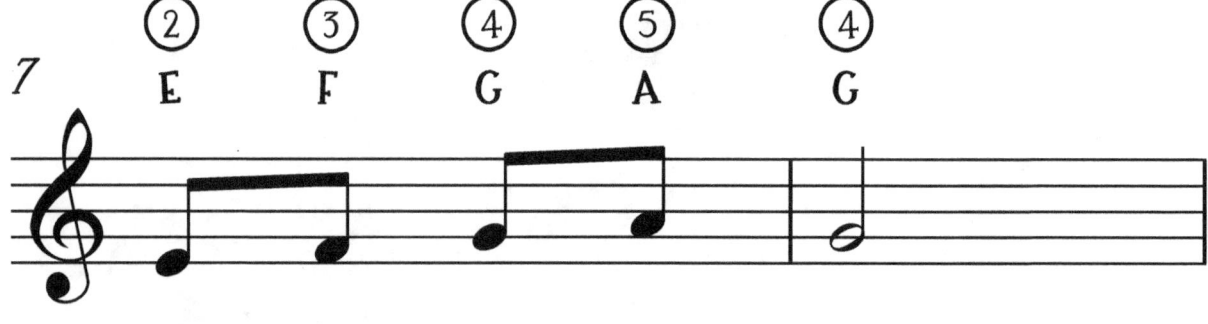

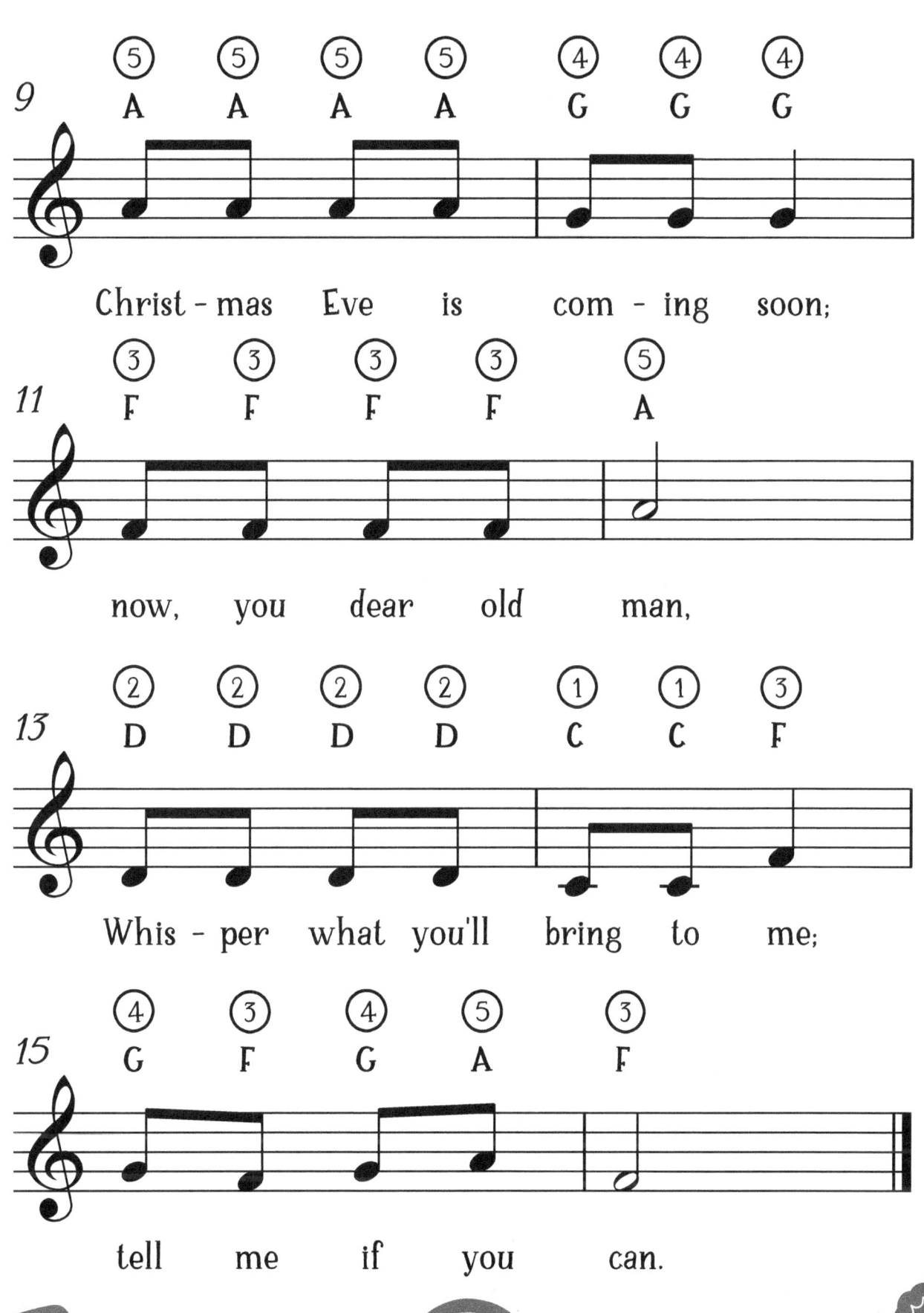

2. When the clock is striking twelve,
   When I'm fast asleep,
   Down the chimney broad and black
   With your pack you'll creep;
   All the stockings you will find
   Hanging in a row;
   Mine will be the shortest one;
   You'll be sure to know.

3. Johnny wants a pair of skates;
   Susy wants a dolly
   Nellie wants a story book,
   She thinks dolls are folly
   As for me, my little brain
   Isn't very bright;
   Choose for me, dear Santa Claus,
   What you think is right.

USEFUL TIP

In this song you will need to move your hand a little to the left or right to reach all the notes. There are two positions: one starts with finger 1 on C, the other with finger 1 on D (and finger 5 on A).

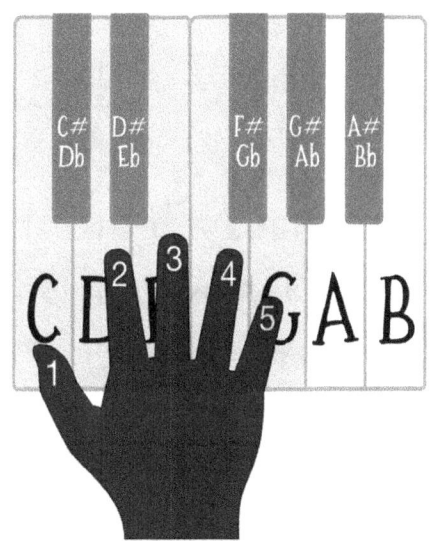 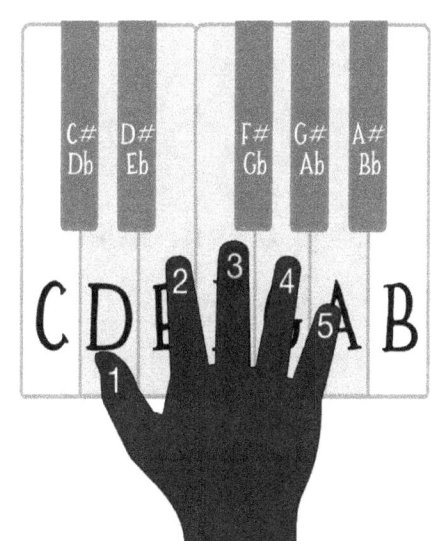

You will need to start with finger 1 on D (and finger 5 on A). Then when you get to the fifth measure you will need to move your hand slightly to the left to play the D with finger 2. This way you will end up in C position.

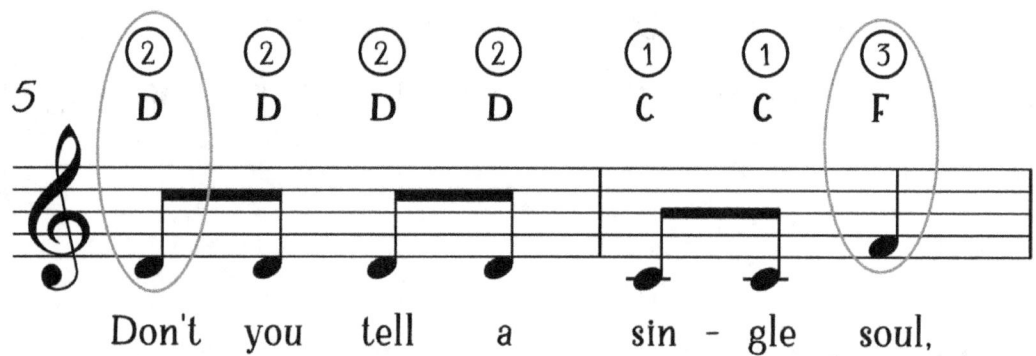

In measure 6, you will need to stretch your hand a bit to the right to play the F. This is an easy way to return to D position. Do exactly the same thing in thirteenth and fourteenth measures.

Jesus, Joy of Man's Desiring

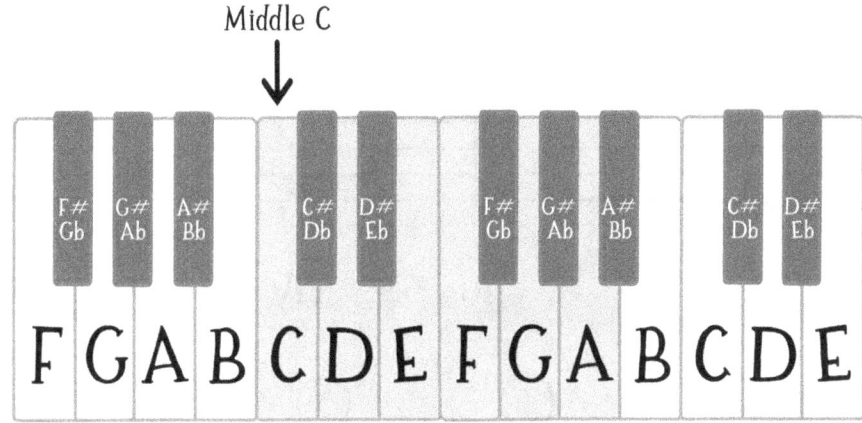

USEFUL TIP at the end of the song

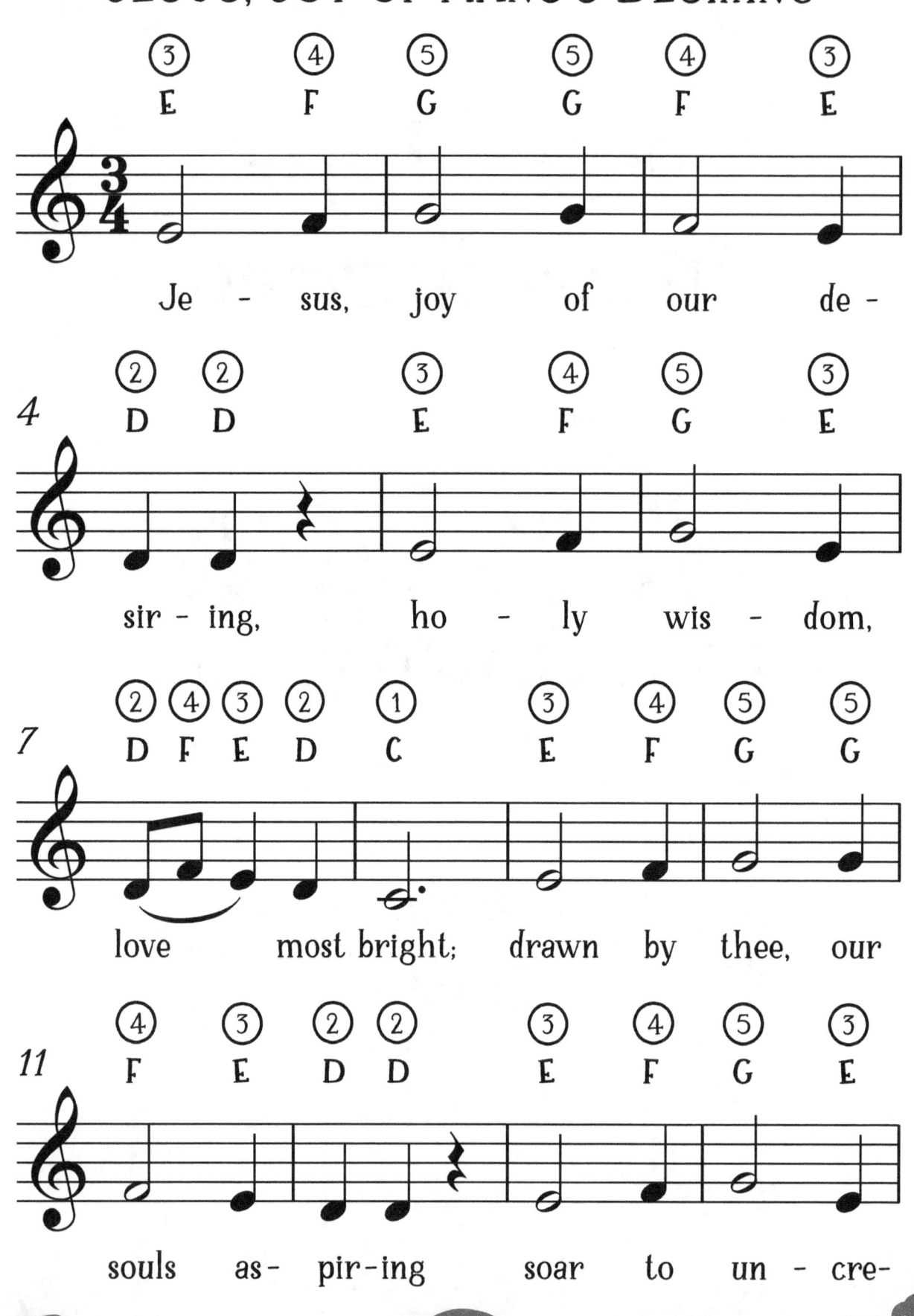

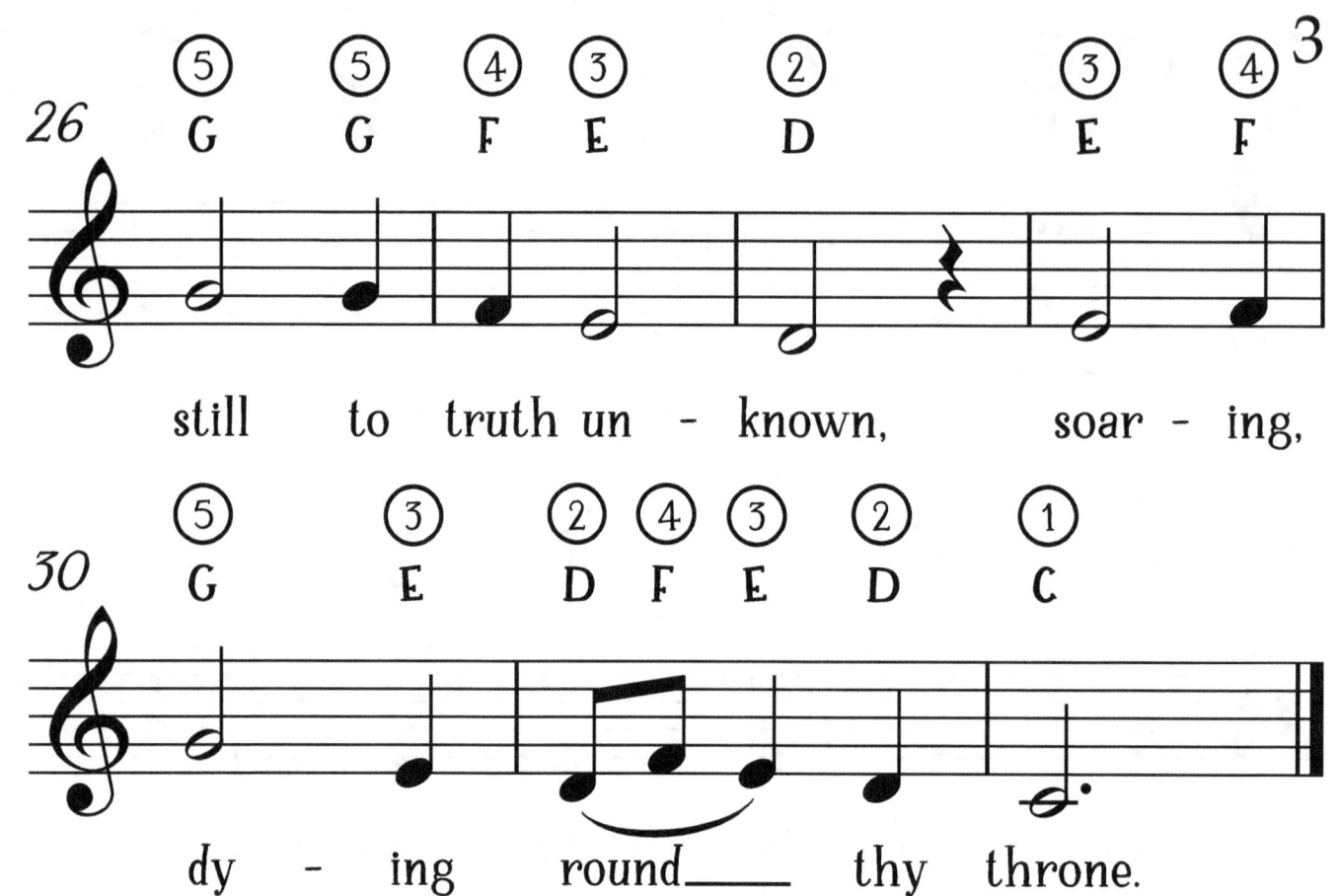

2. Through the way where hope is guiding,
   Hark, what peaceful music rings;
   Where the flock, in thee confiding,
   Drink of joy from deathless springs.
   Theirs is beauty's fairest pleasure;
   Theirs is wisdom's holiest treasure.
   Thou dost ever lead thine own
   In the love of joys unknown.

There are a couple of things in this song that you should pay attention to.

On the second page you can see two different notes near each other with the same finger number.

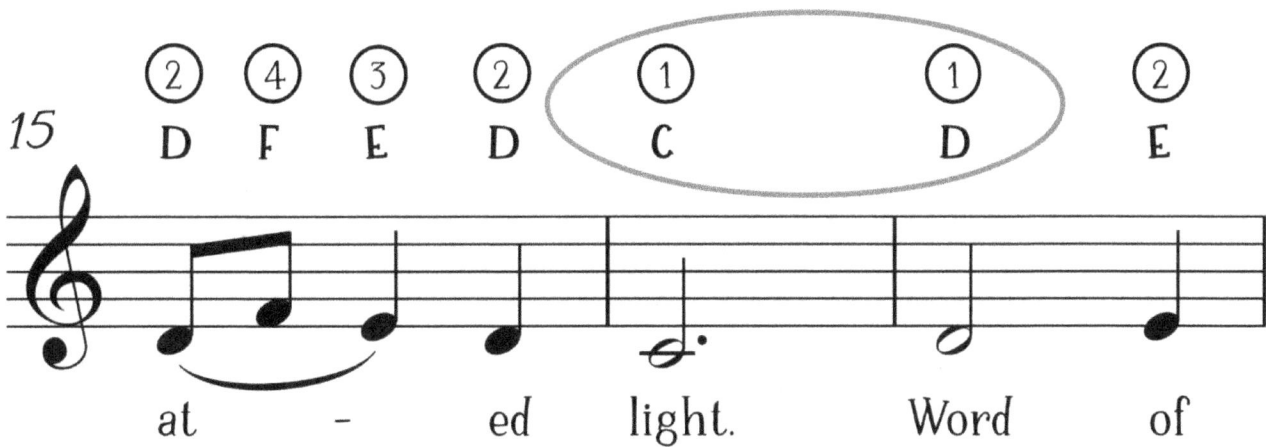

When you release the C you should move your hand to the right so finger 1 can now play D. This way notes that come after will be right under your fingers.

There are also a few more things that you might have noticed. Some notes are connected by a curved line. This line is called a slur.

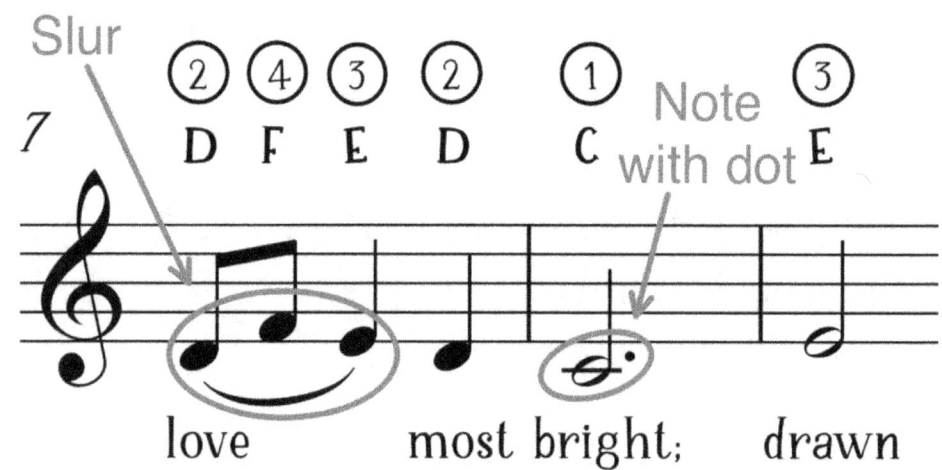

When you see a slur, you should play these notes smoothly. Each note should be played after another with no interruptions or even the smallest pause. You shouldn't raise your hand up above the keyboard while playing them. Your finger should hold one key down until you press the next one.

Another thing you will see occasionally in this song is a small dot near the head of a half note. This dot makes the note value longer by one half. So instead of holding the note for two beats, it should be held for three. This way it is possible to have only one note for a whole measure when the time signature is in 3/4.

I Saw Three Ships

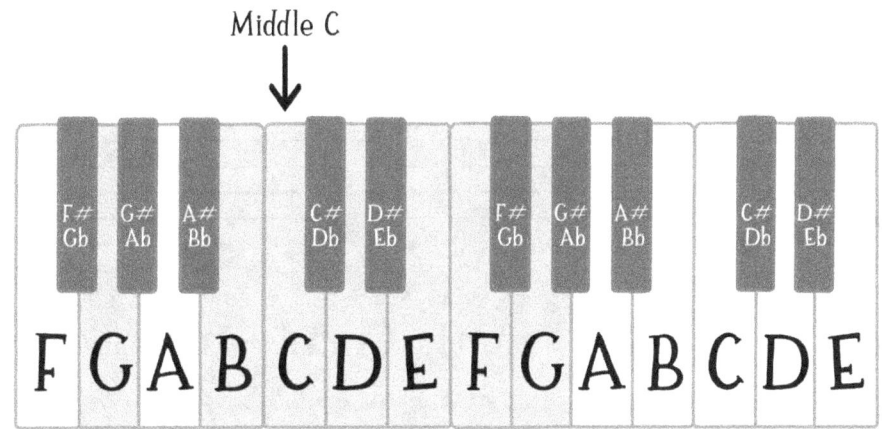

USEFUL TIP at the end of the song

I SAW THREE SHIPS

2. And who was in those ships all three,
   On Christmas Day, on Christmas Day?
   And who was in those ships all three,
   On Christmas Day in the morning?

3. Our Saviour Christ and his lady,
   On Christmas Day, on Christmas Day;
   Our Saviour Christ and his ladye,
   On Christmas Day in the morning.

4. Pray whither sailed those ships all three,
   On Christmas Day, on Christmas Day?
   Pray whither sailed those ships all three,
   On Christmas Day in the morning?

5. O they sailed into Bethlehem,
   On Christmas Day, on Christmas Day;
   O they sailed into Bethlehem,
   On Christmas Day in the morning.

6. And all the bells on Earth shall ring,
   On Christmas Day, on Christmas Day;
   And all the bells on Earth shall ring,
   On Christmas Day in the morning.

7. And all the angels in Heaven shall sing,
   On Christmas Day, on Christmas Day;
   And all the angels in Heaven shall sing,
   On Christmas Day in the morning.

8. And all the souls on Earth shall sing,
   On Christmas Day, on Christmas Day;
   And all the souls on Earth shall sing,
   On Christmas Day in the morning.

USEFUL TIP

Stay attentive to the fingering in this song:

1.   In the first two full measures, you play the E with finger 4, then with finger 3. The same thing happens in the third line of the song, because these measures are repeated.

2.   Between measures 4 and 5 there are two different notes that you should play with the same finger. Just move your hand slightly to the left to play the D note.

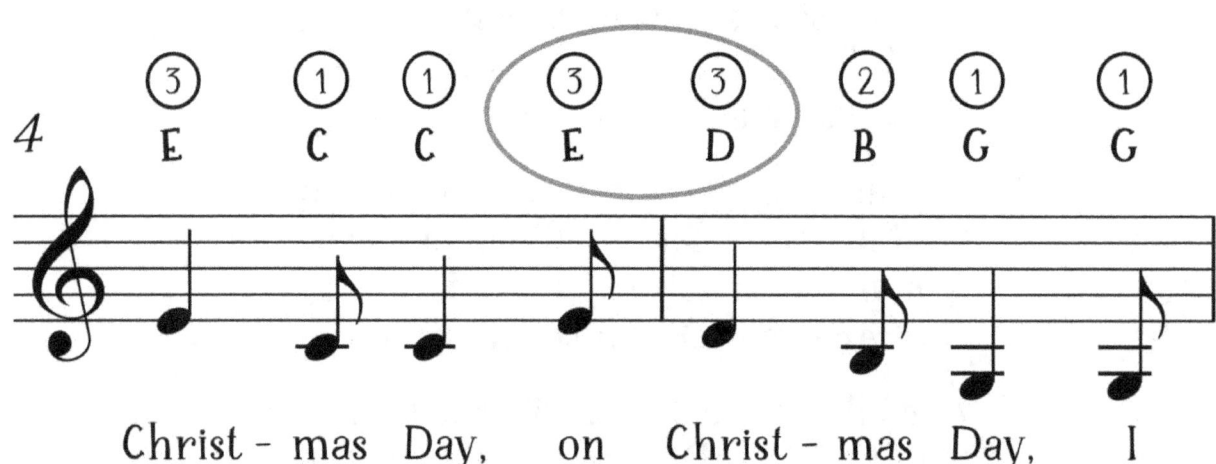

Chapter 2

Bring a Torch, Jeanette Isabella

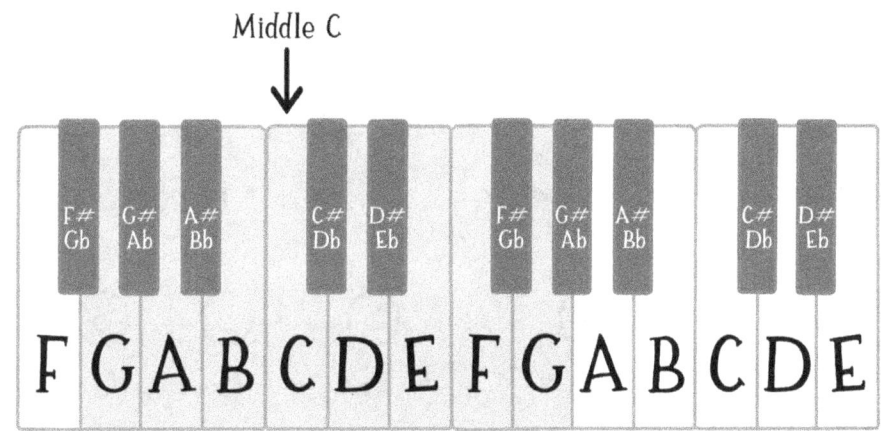

BRING A TORCH, JEANETTE, ISABELLA

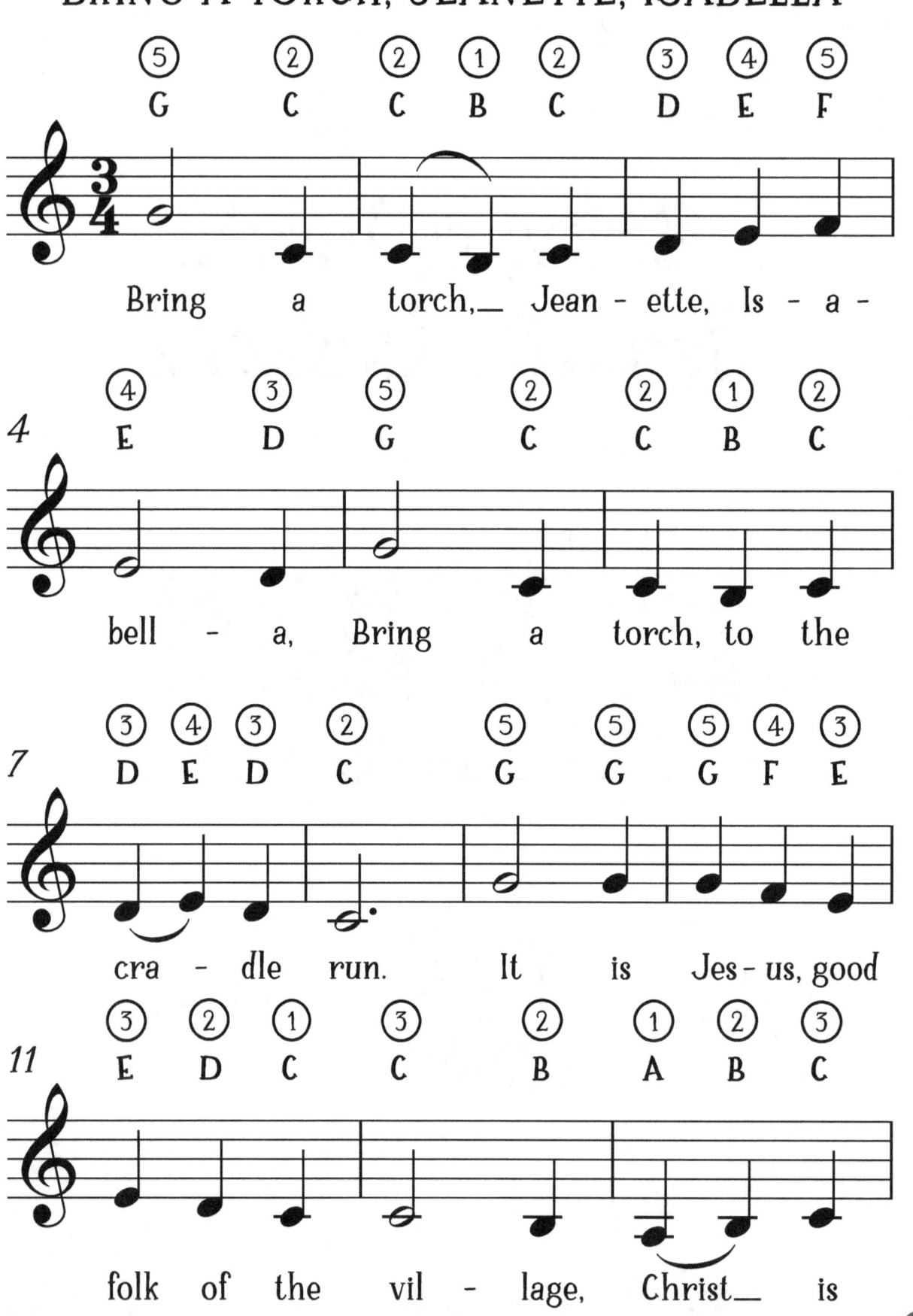

2. It is wrong when the child is sleeping,
   It is wrong to talk so loud;
   Silence, all, as you gather around,
   Lest your noise should waken Jesus.
   Hush! hush! see how fast He slumbers;
   Hush! hush! see how fast He sleeps!

3. Softly to the little stable.
   Softly for a moment come;
   Look and see how charming is Jesus,
   How He is warm, His cheeks are rosy.
   Hush! hush! see how the child is sleeping;
   Hush! hush! see how He smiles in dreams.

USEFUL TIP

Watch out! There are plenty of finger changes and different hand positions in this song:

1. Between measures 4 and 5 your hand needs to "jump" to the right so you will be able to reach G with finger 5.

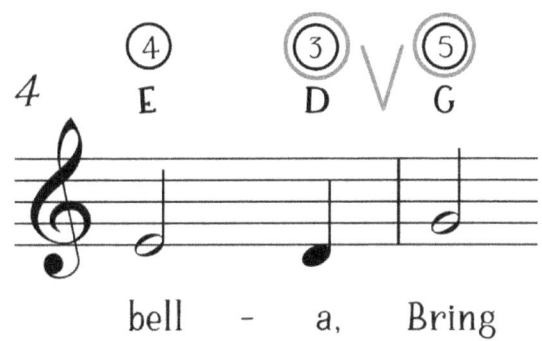

2. Between measures 11 and 12 when you play C with finger 1 and then with finger 3, you also should move your hand to the left. This will help you to reach the lower notes in the next several measures.

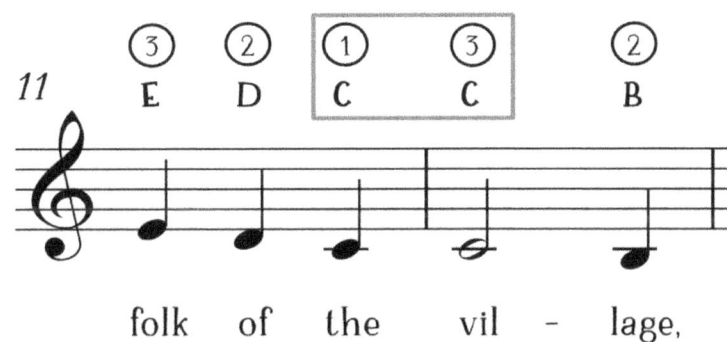

3. Keep an eye out for a similar thing in measure 15 on the F. This time, move your hand slightly to the right. And this hand position will work till the end of the song.

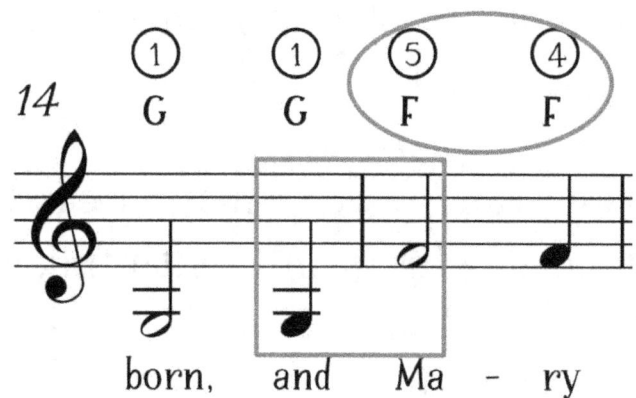

4. Right before this there is a wide leap from G to F. So you need to stretch your hand to the right while you are still playing G.

We Wish You a Merry Christmas

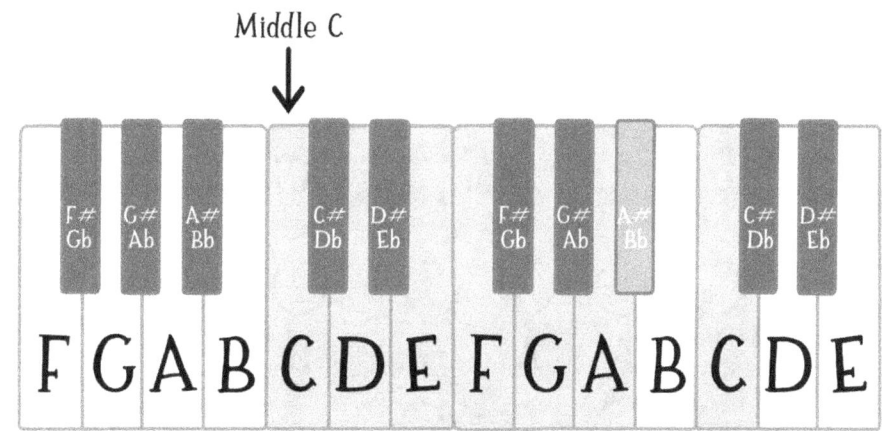

USEFUL TIP at the end of the song

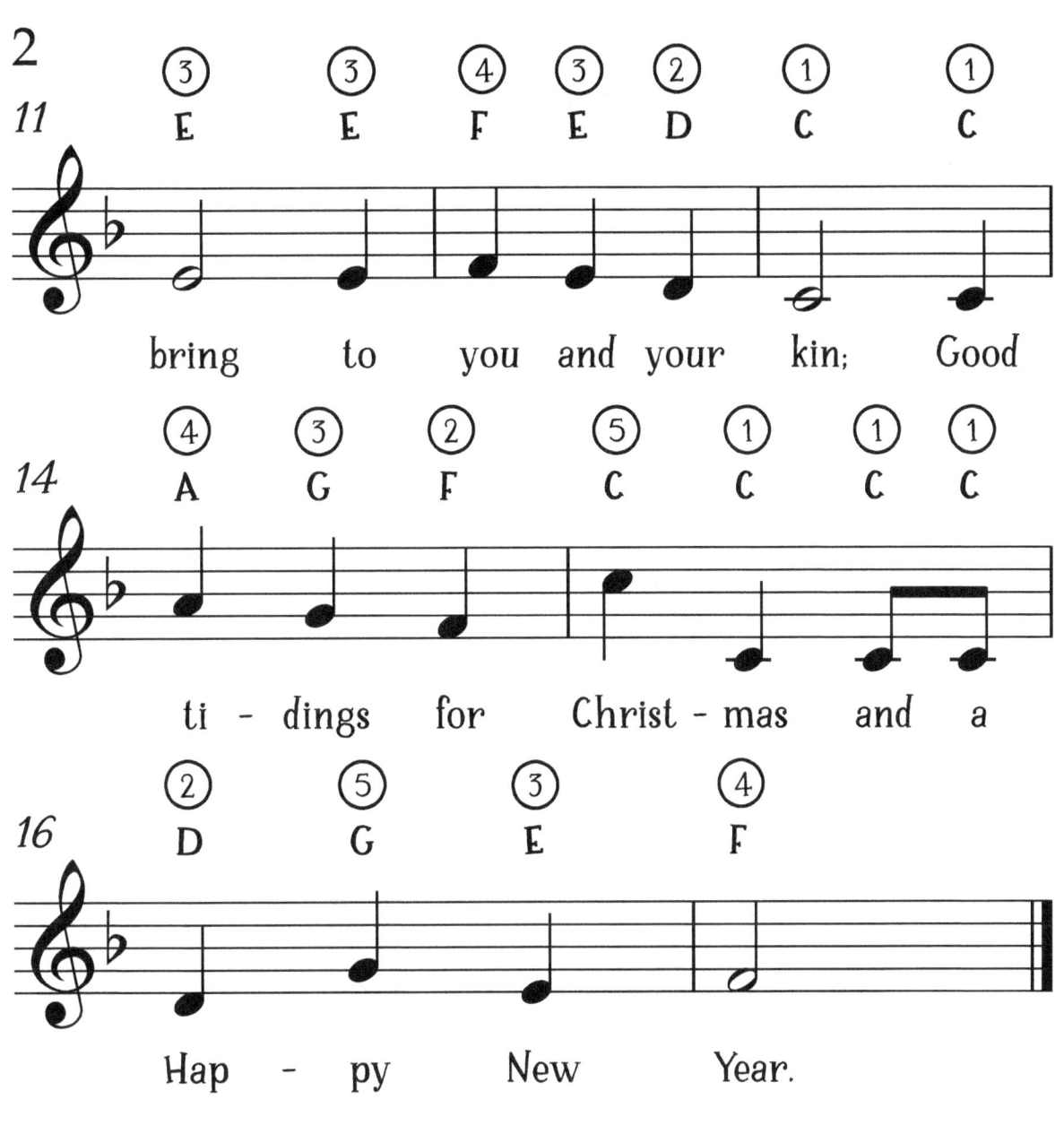

2. Oh, bring us a figgy pudding, (x 3)
   and a cup of good cheer!
   Good tidings ...

3. We won't go until we get some, (x 3)
   so bring some out here.
   Good tidings ...

4. We wish you a Merry Christmas, (x 3)
   and a Happy New Year.
   Good tidings ...

USEFUL TIP

Do you remember what it means when a flat (or sharp) is near the treble clef sign? When you see this, you will play that sharp or flat instead of the white note for the whole song. In this song we have a B flat. So each time you see B, play the black key that is to the left of the B-his is B flat.

We Three Kings of Orient Are

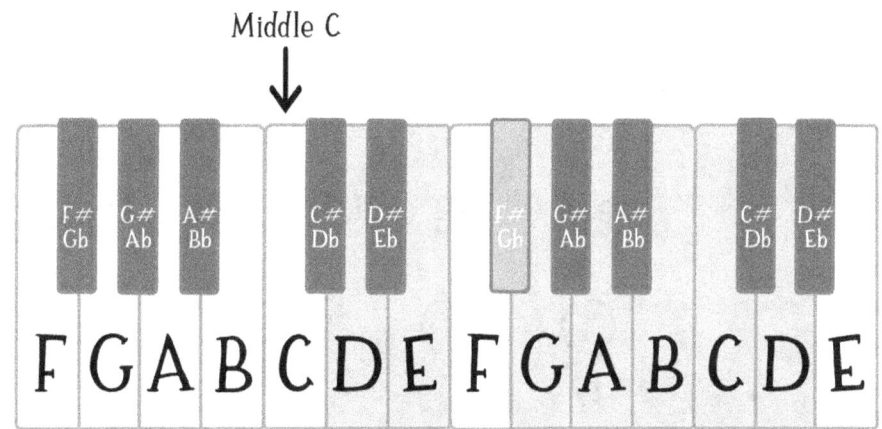

USEFUL TIP at the end of the song

WE THREE KINGS OF ORIENT ARE

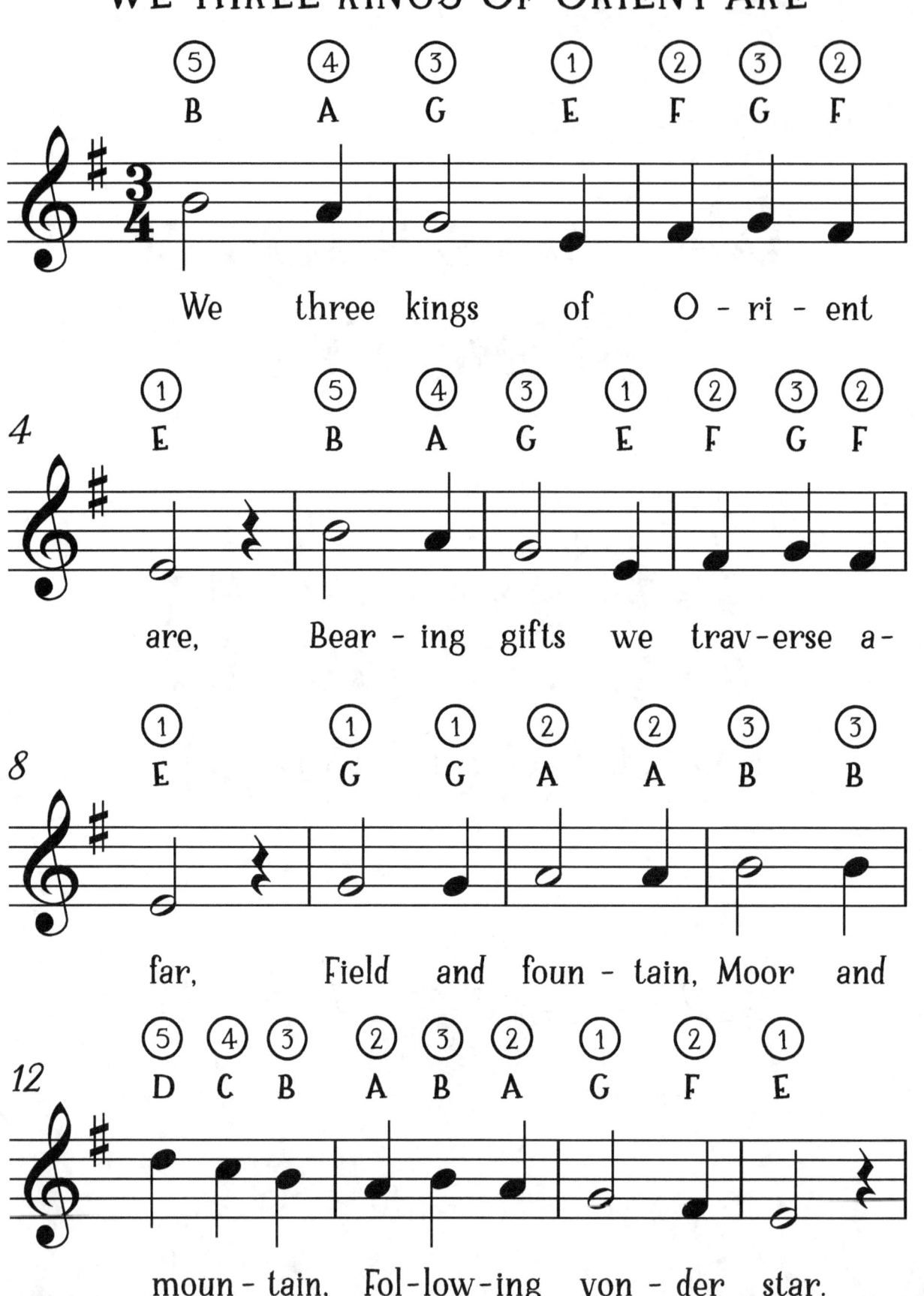

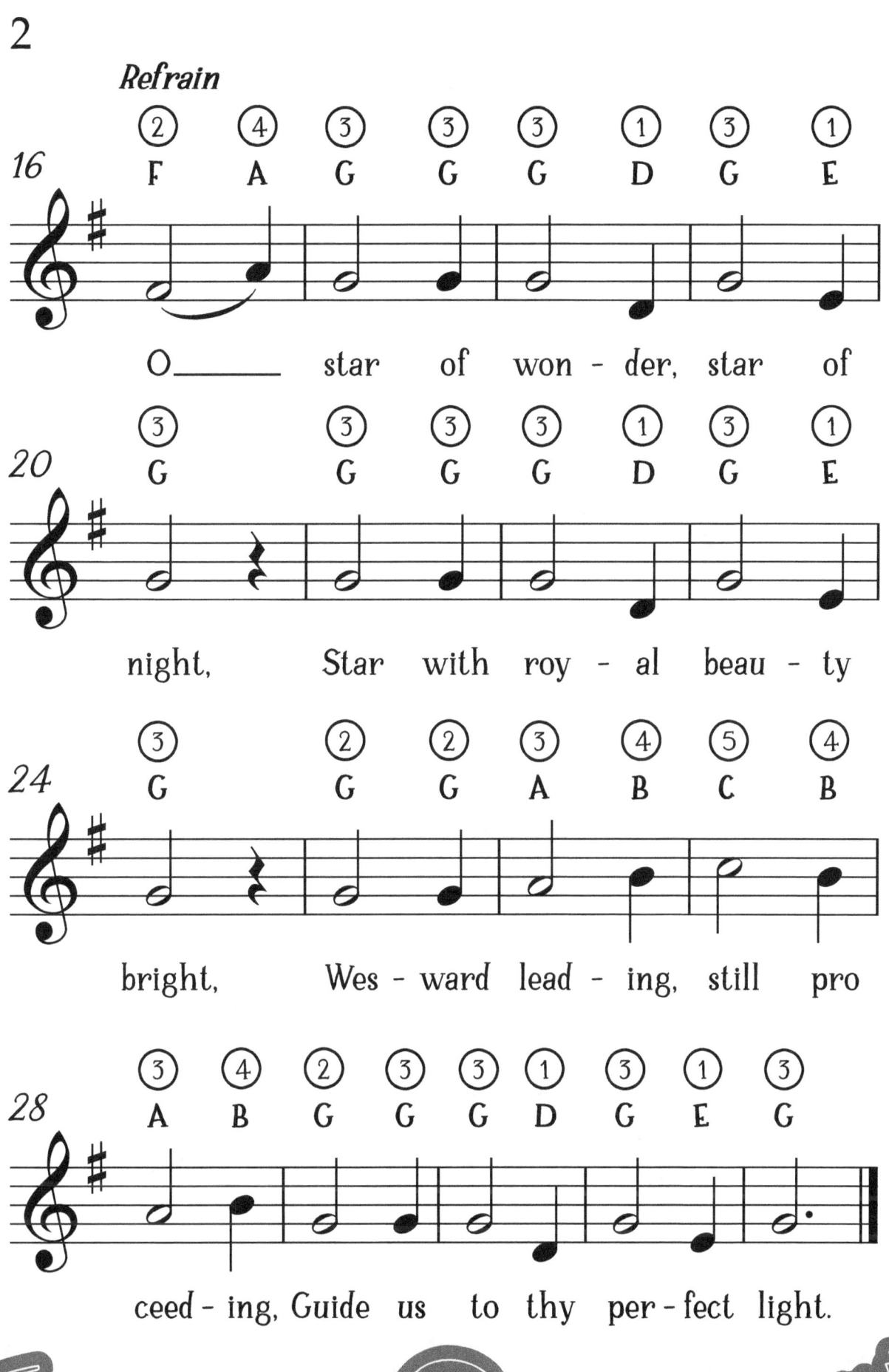

2. Born a King on Bethlehem's plain,
   Gold I bring to crown him again,
   King forever, ceasing never,
   Over us all to reign.

Refrain

3. Frankincense to offer have I;
   Incense owns a Deity nigh;
   Prayer and praising, voices raising,
   Worshiping God on high.

Refrain

4. Myrrh is mine; its bitter perfume
   Breathes a life of gathering gloom;
   Sorrowing, sighing, bleeding, dying,
   Sealed in the stone-cold tomb.

Refrain

5. Glorious now behold him arise;
   King and God and sacrifice:
   Alleluia, Alleluia,
   Sounds through the earth and skies.

Refrain

Pay attention to the F sharp near the treble clef sign. Remember, that means you need to play F sharp (the black key to the right of F) every time you see an F in the music.

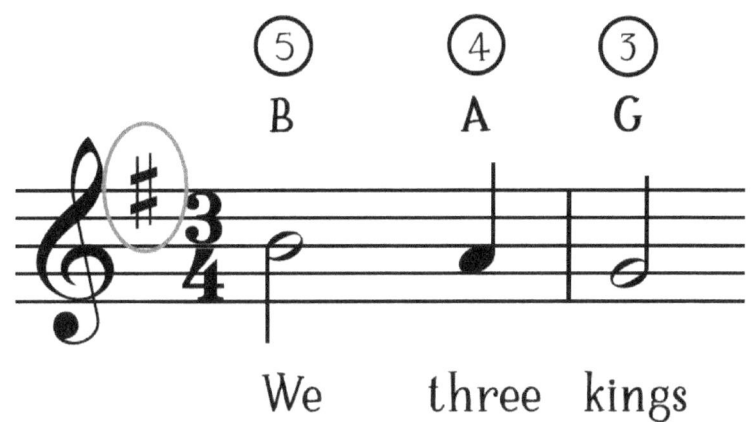

There is also one more high note in this song. It sits on the fourth line and is the D above the higher C.

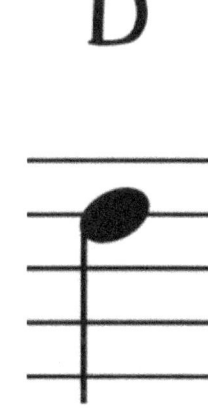

This is where it is on the keyboard:

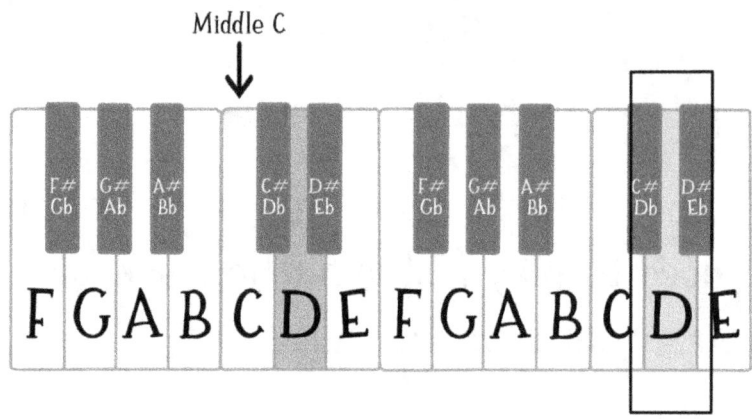

One last thing-pay close attention to the fingering!

1. In the third line make sure you move your hand a bit to the right during the quarter rest:

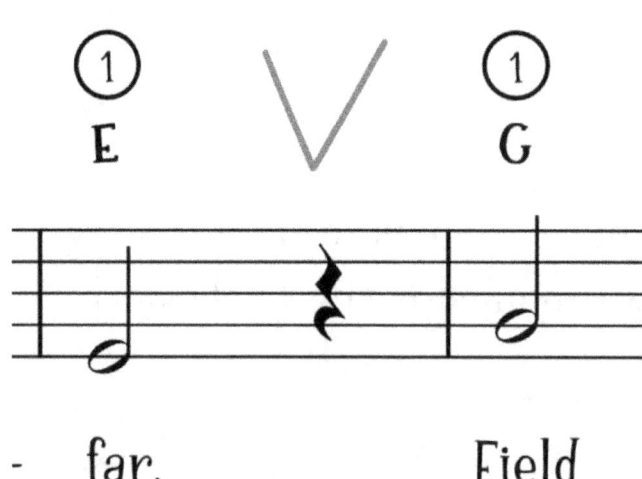

2. In measure 14 you should move finger 2 over finger 1 while you are still holding G. Now you can reach E.

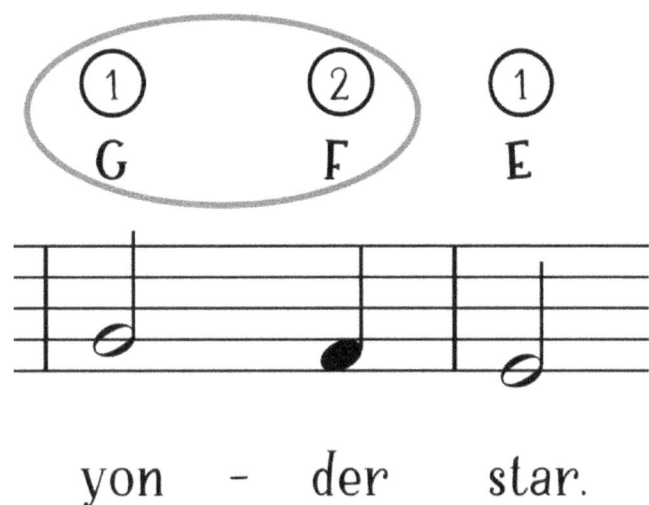

yon - der   star.

3. And finally, watch for places when the fingers are changing while you are repeating a note.

Chapter 3

If you flipped through this chapter, you may have already noticed that from now on you will play songs with both of your hands. The upper staff shows the notes for your right hand, and the lower staff shows the notes for your left hand. Both of them have treble clefs at the beginning. In other song books, the left hand will often play in the bass clef, but in this book, we will focus on the treble clef.

Now that you have ten fingers to play with, you might notice that fingerings are easier to play. The new challenge is learning to pass the melody between your hands, but you can do it! Start slow, and try singing along. It will really help-and put you in the Christmas spirit!

Coventry Carol

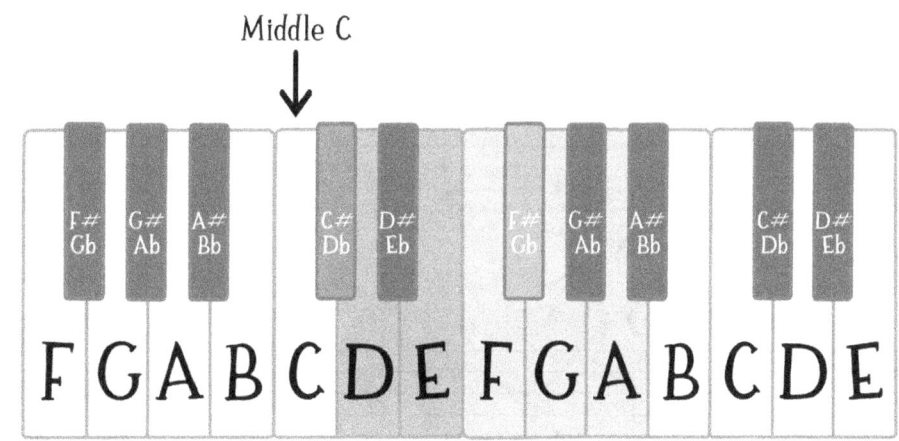

COVENTRY CAROL

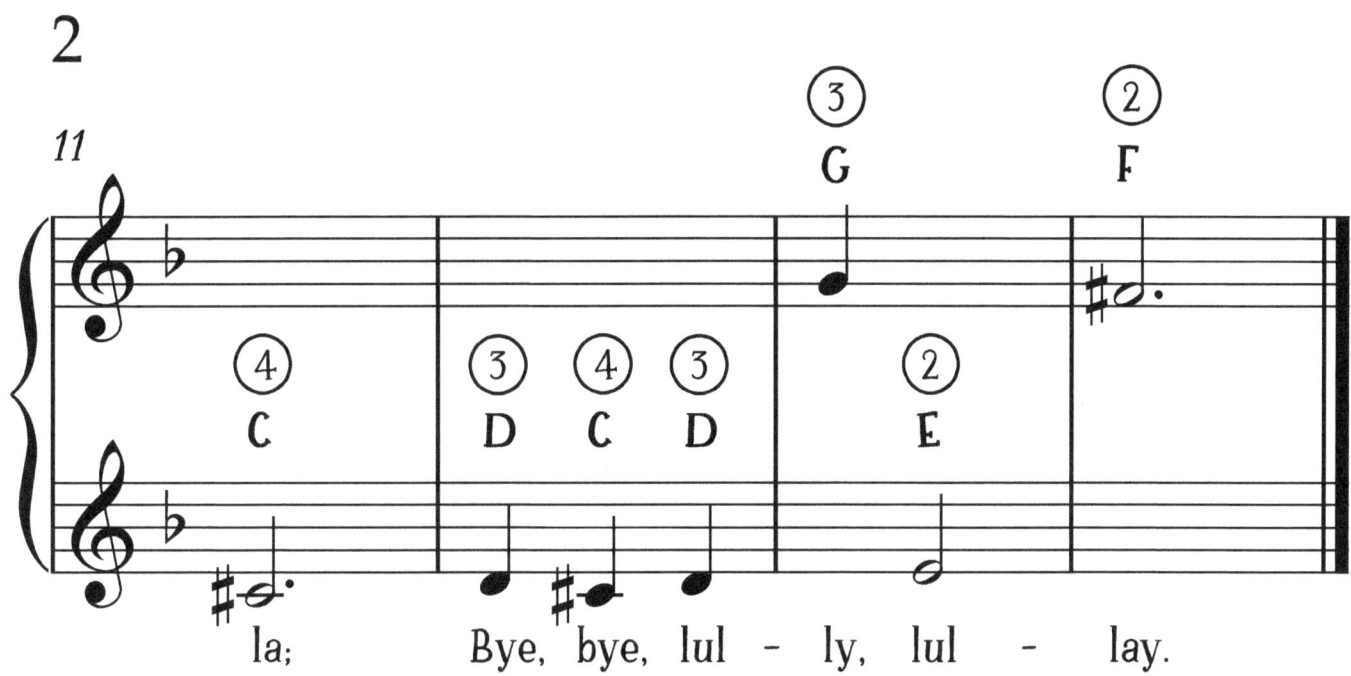

2. O sisters too, how may we do
   For to preserve this day,
   This poor youngling,
   For whom we sing
   Bye, bye, lully, lullay?

3. Herod the King in his raging
   Charged he hath this day,
   His men of might
   In his own sight,
   All children young to slay.

4. That woe is me, poor Child, for Thee
   And ever mourn and say,
   For Thy parting,
   Nor say nor sing
   Bye, bye, lully, lullay.

USEFUL TIP

In this song you have B flat in the key signature. Remember to play B flat (the black key below the B) each time you see B in the music.

But look here!

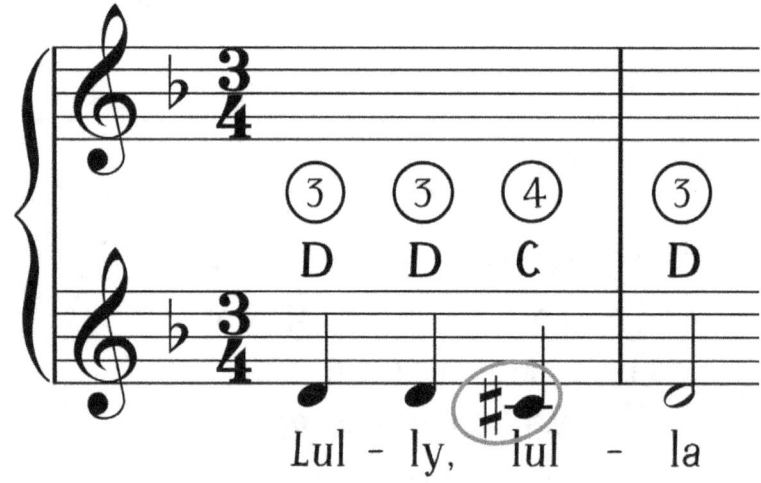

There is a sharp symbol near the C each time it shows up in this song. But it is not near the clef! That's because in music we can't have both sharps and flats in the key signature. So in this song you will always have B flat and C sharp (the black key that is to the right of C).

Look sharp! There's another-sharp, that is: in the last measure you will also have F sharp-don't forget.

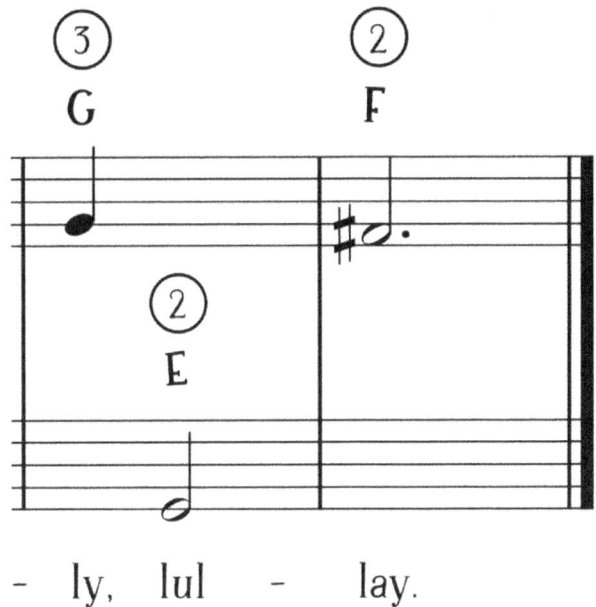

- ly, lul - lay.

You can find it the same way as C sharp: it is the closest black key above F.

Dotted rhythm

Do you remember what the dot near the note head does? It increases the note's value by half. In the third and eighth measures you can see what we call "dotted rhythm."

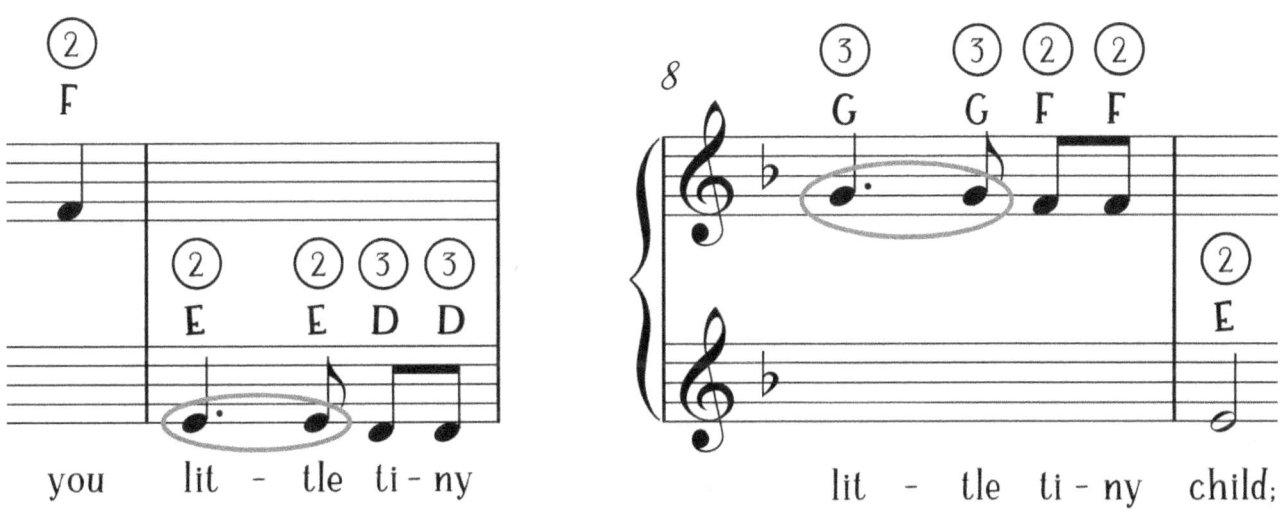

To help you get this tricky rhythm, you can practice with this simple exercise.

Clap 4 eighth notes, saying the syllable "ta" on each of them.

Then say it in the same way, but clap only on the first and last notes.

Then try to hold the first ta.

This is how the dotted rhythm sounds!

The First Noel

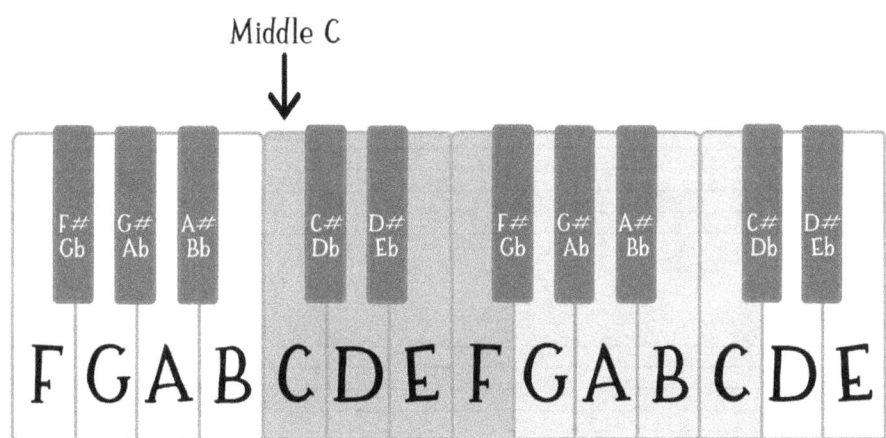

THE FIRST NOEL

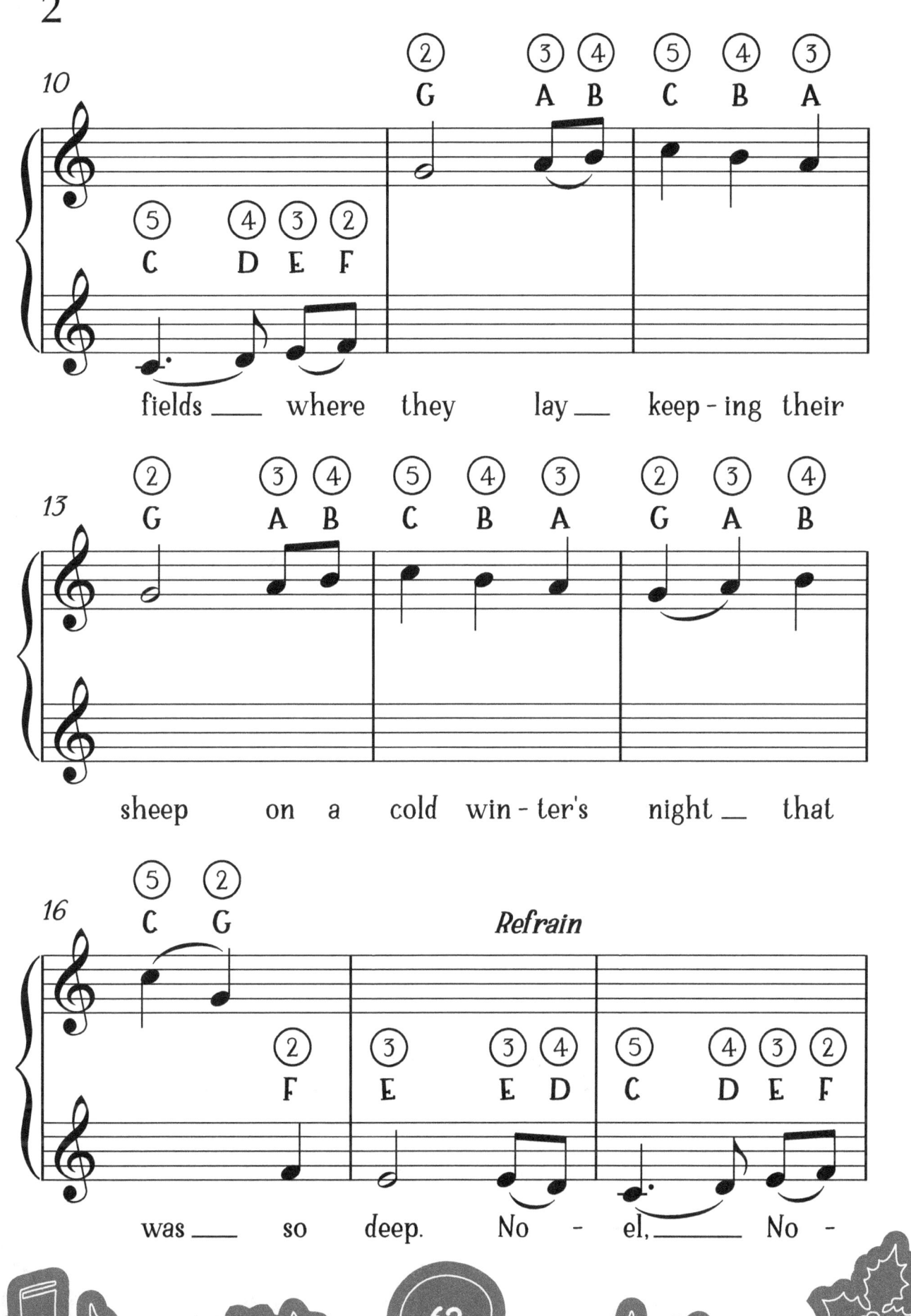

2. They looked up and saw a star
   Shining in the east beyond them far;
   And to the earth it gave great light,
   And so it continued both day and night.

Refrain

3 And by the light of that same star
   Three wise men came from country far;
   To seek for a king was their intent,
   And to follow the star wherever it went.

Refrain

4

4. This star drew nigh to the northwest;
   O'er Bethlehem it took its rest,
   And there it did both stop and stay,
   Right over the place where Jesus lay.

Refrain

5. Then entered in those wise men three,
   Full reverently upon their knee,
   And offered there in his presence
   Their gold, and myrrh, and frankincense.

Refrain

6. Then let us all with one accord
   Sing praises to our heavenly Lord,
   That hath made heaven and earth of nought,
   And with his blood our life hath bought.

Refrain

God Rest You Merry, Gentlemen

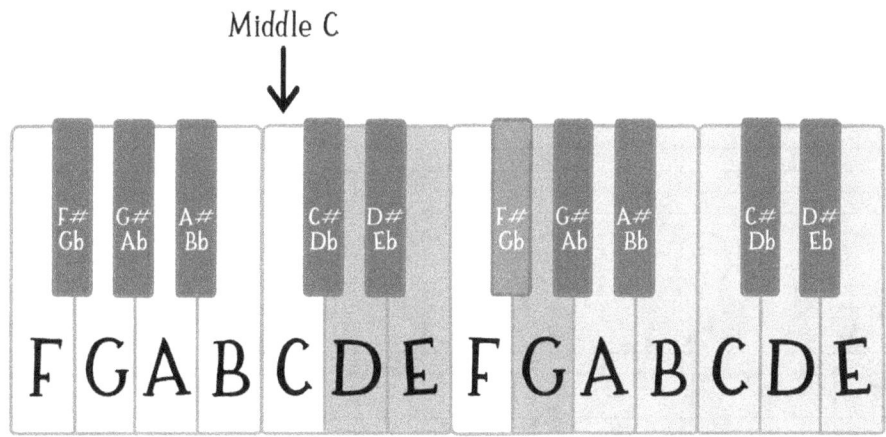

GOD REST YOU MERRY, GENTLEMEN

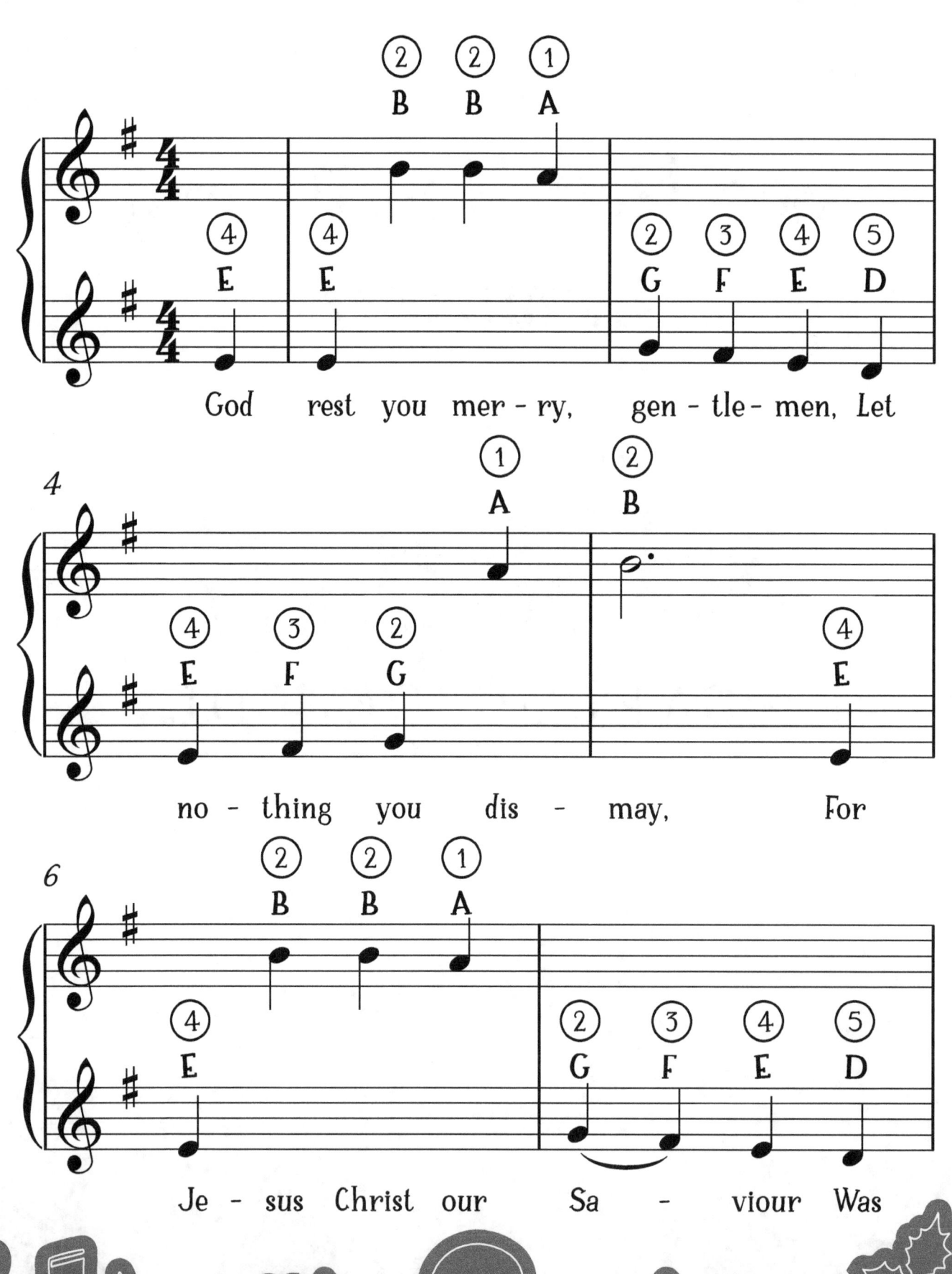

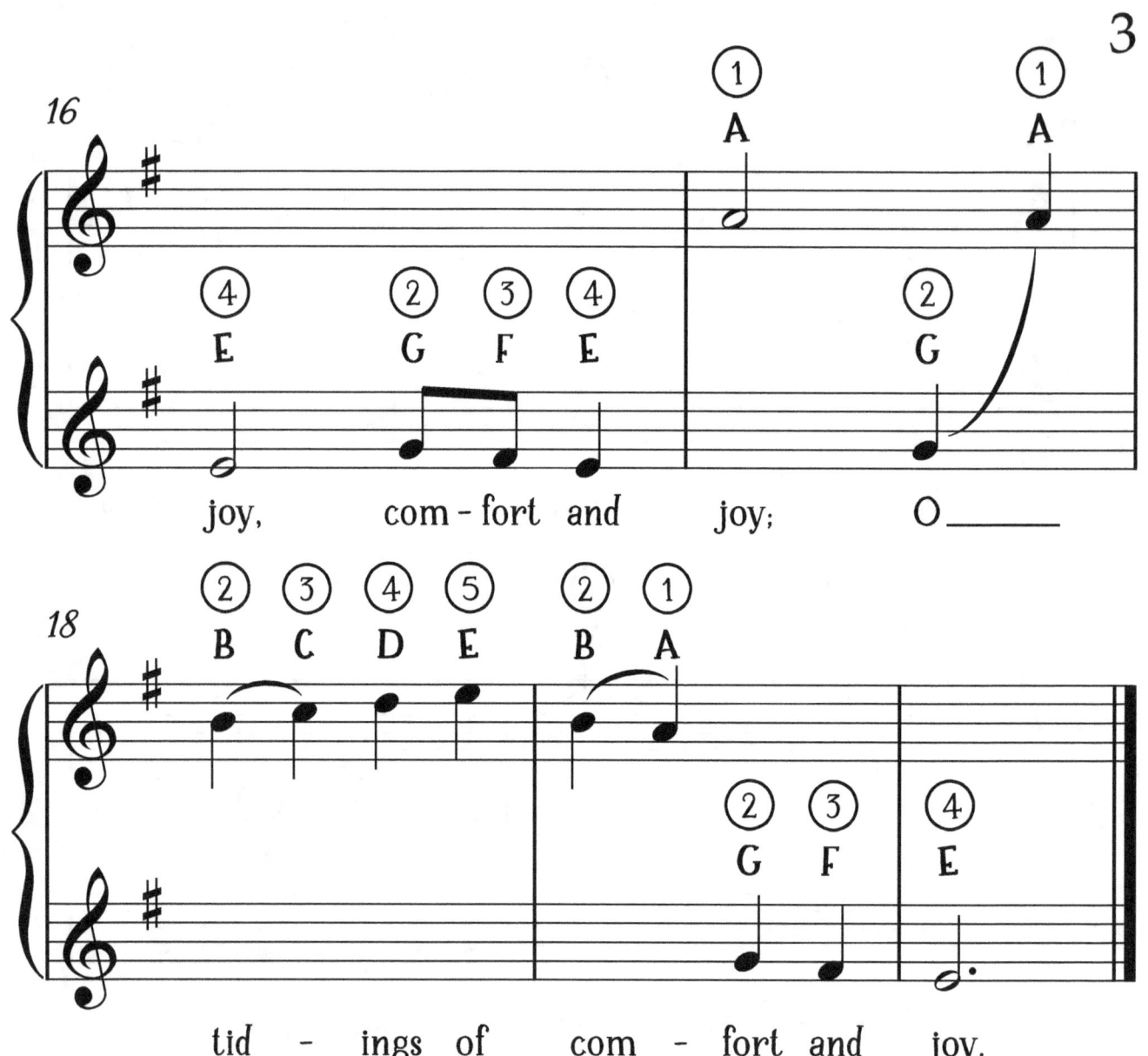

2. From God our heav'nly Father
a blessed angel came
and unto certain shepherds
brought tidings of the same;
how that in Bethlehem was born
the Son of God by name.

Refrain

3. "Fear not," then said the angel,
   "Let nothing you affright;
   this day is born a Savior
   of a pure virgin bright,
   to free all those who trust in Him
   from Satan's pow'r and might."

Refrain

4. The shepherds at those tidings
   rejoiced much in mind,
   and left their flocks afeeding,
   in tempest, storm, and wind,
   and went to Bethlehem straightway,
   this blessed Babe to find.

Refrain

5. Now to the Lord sing praises
   all you within this place,
   and with true love and brotherhood
   each other now embrace;
   this holy tide of Christmas
   all other doth deface.

Refrain

Deck the Halls

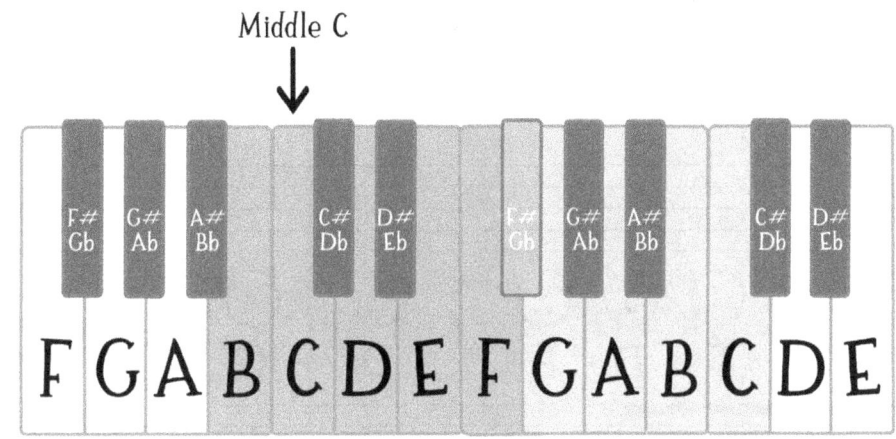

This song is played in a different position than you are used to, so pay close attention to note names and finger numbers to help you play the right notes! In this song, finger number 1 of both hands will rest on F.

DECK THE HALLS

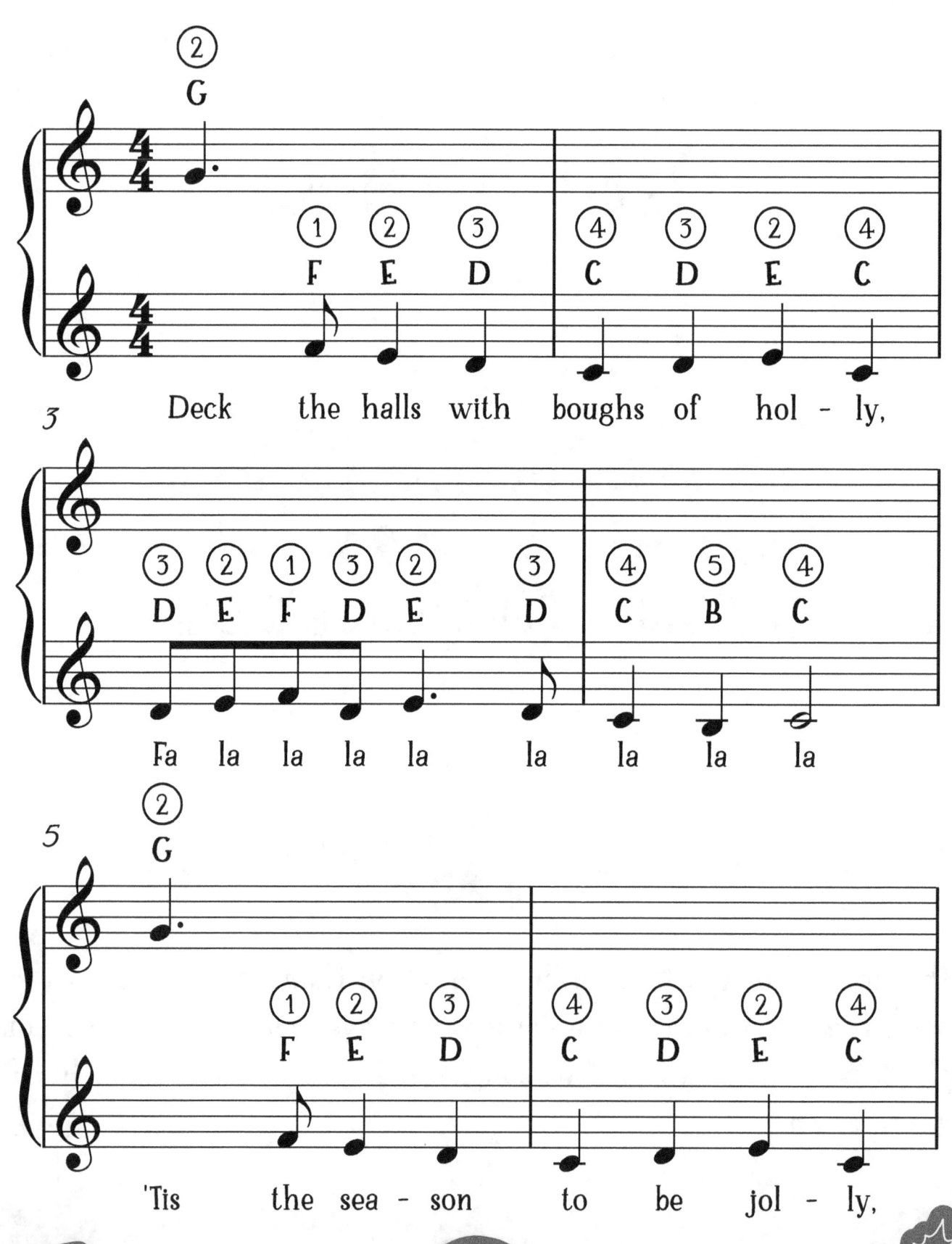

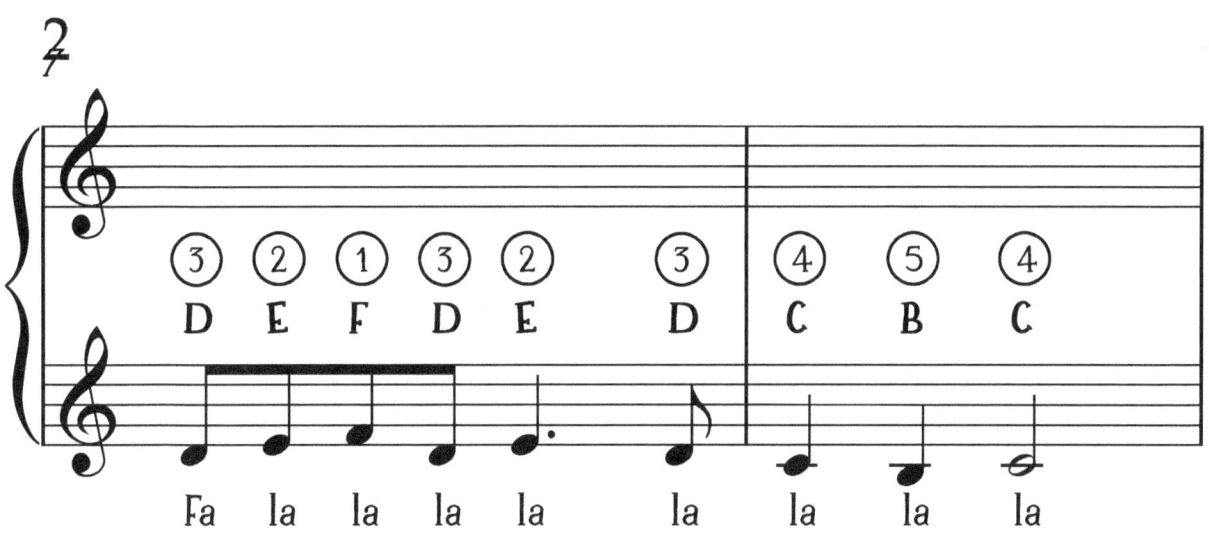
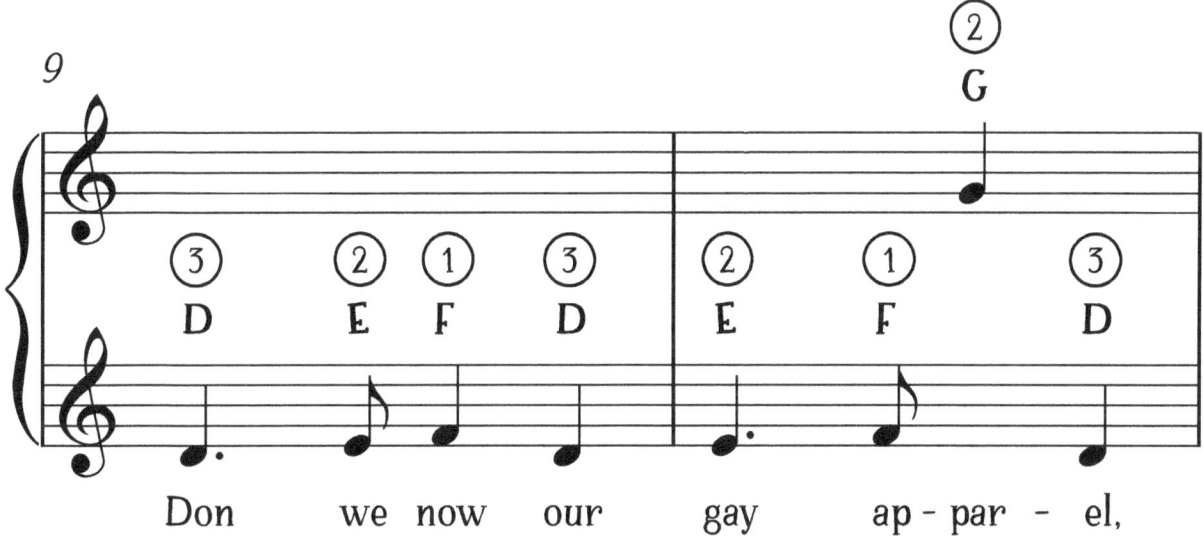
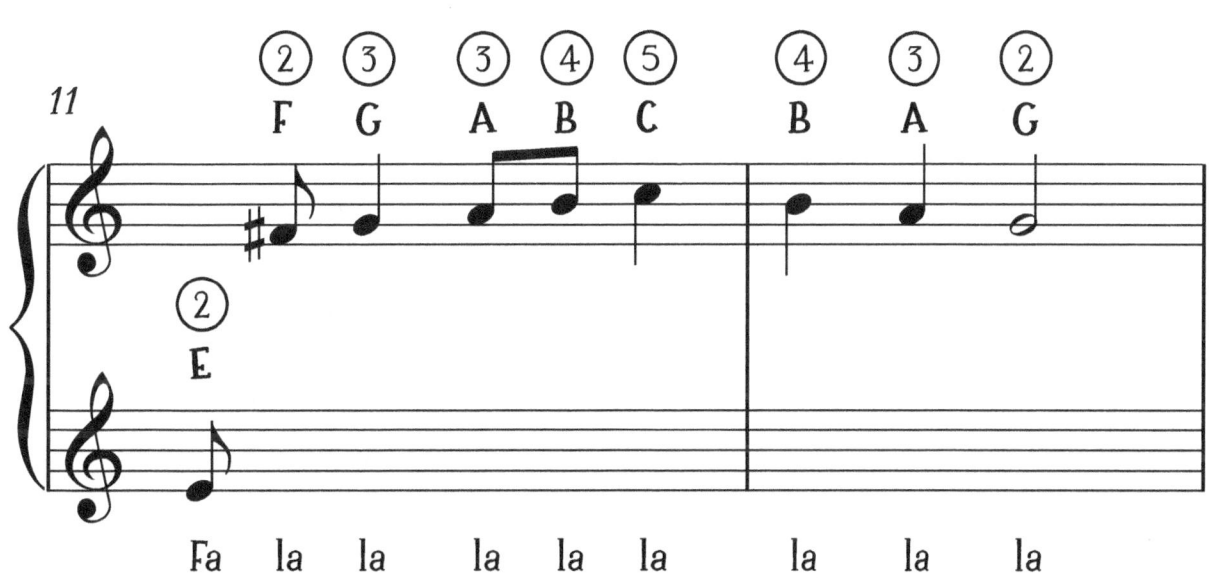

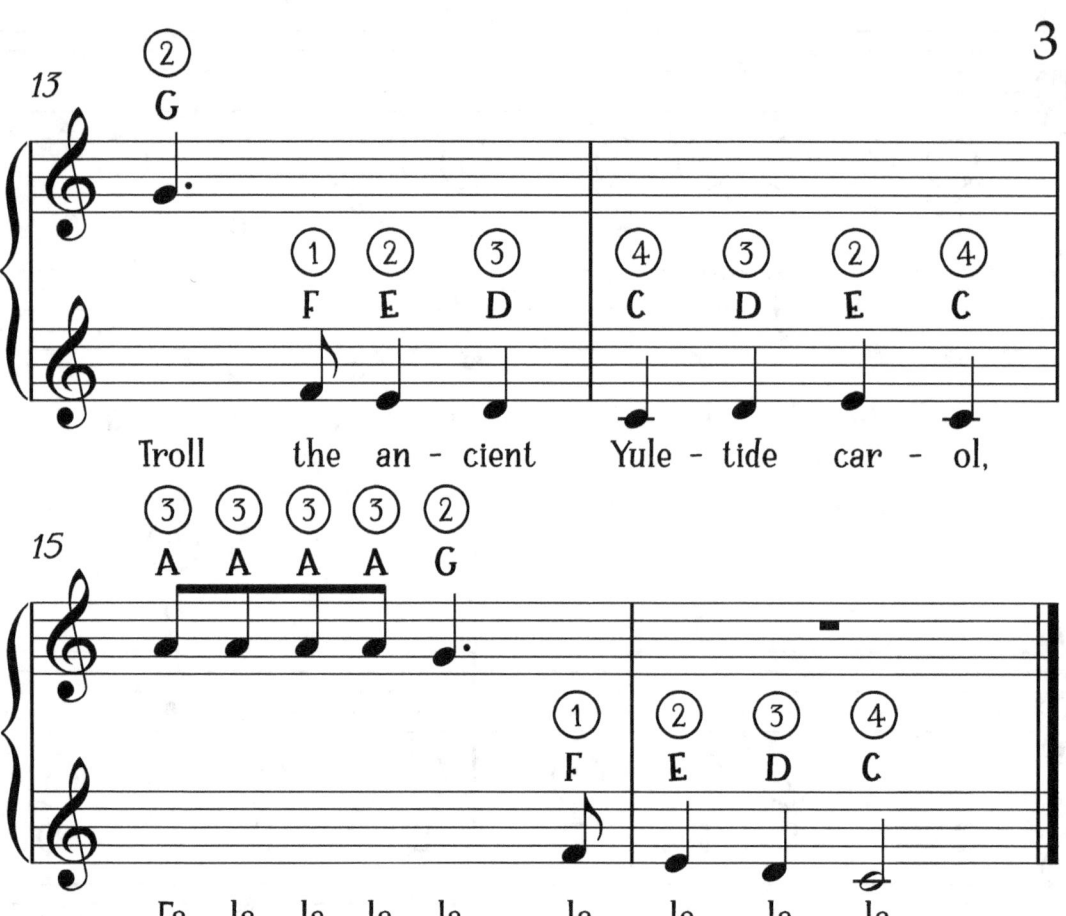

2. See the blazing Yule before us,
   Fa la la la la, la la la.
   Strike the harp and join the chorus,
   Fa la la la la, la la la.
   Follow me in merry measure,
   Fa la la la la, la la la.
   While I tell of Yuletide treasure,
   Fa la la la la, la la la.

3. Fast away the old year passes,
   Fa la la la la, la la la.
   Hail the new, ye lads and lasses,
   Fa la la la la, la la la.
   Sing we joyous all together,
   Fa la la la la, la la la.
   Heedless of the wind and weather,
   Fa la la la la, la la la.

Angels We Have Heard on High

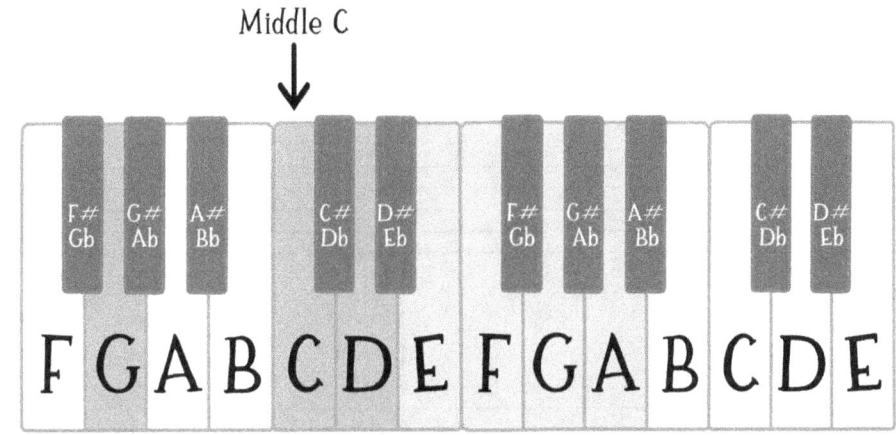

To play this song you should place both hands so finger 1 on each hand will share D.

ANGELS WE HAVE HEARD ON HIGH

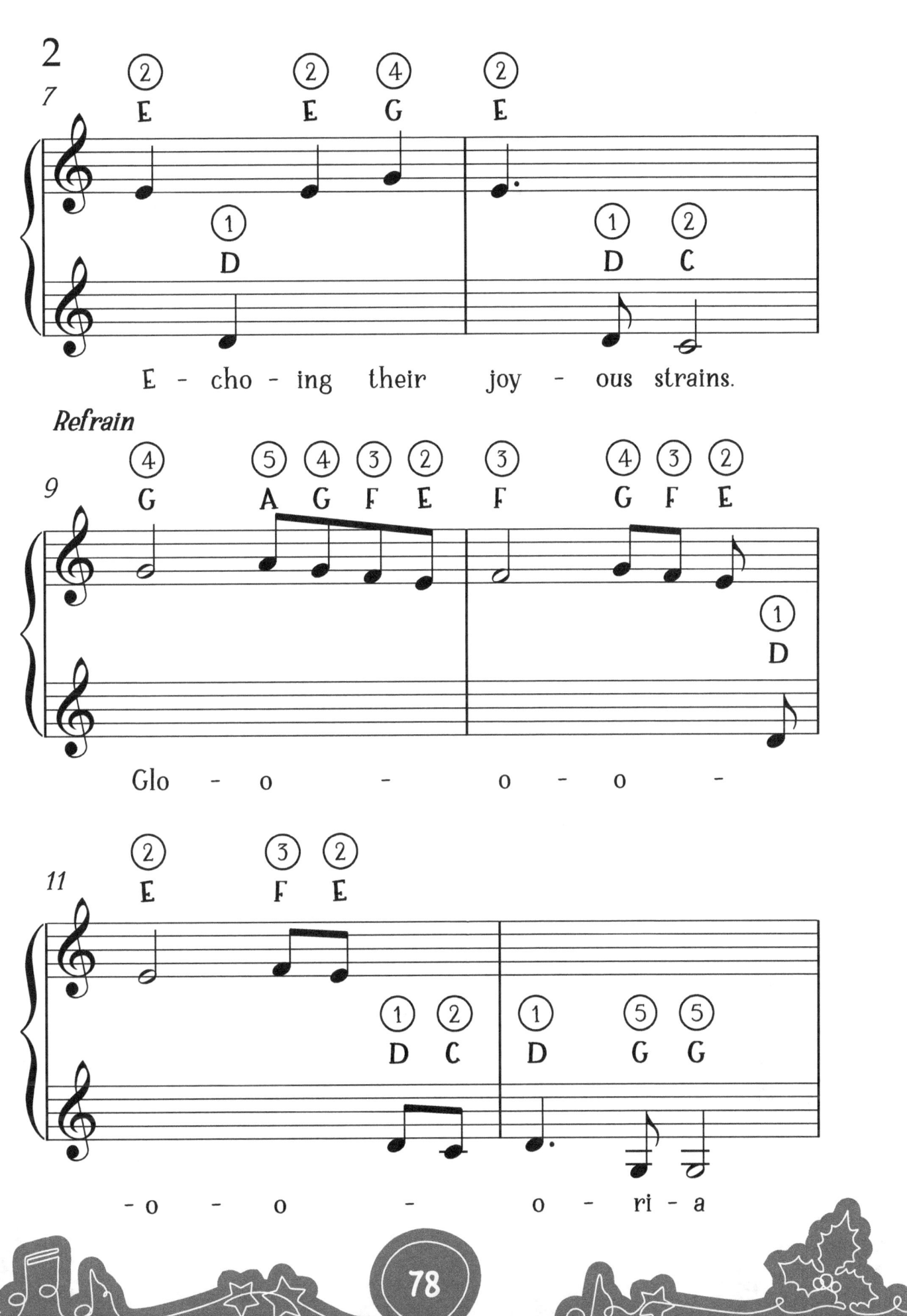

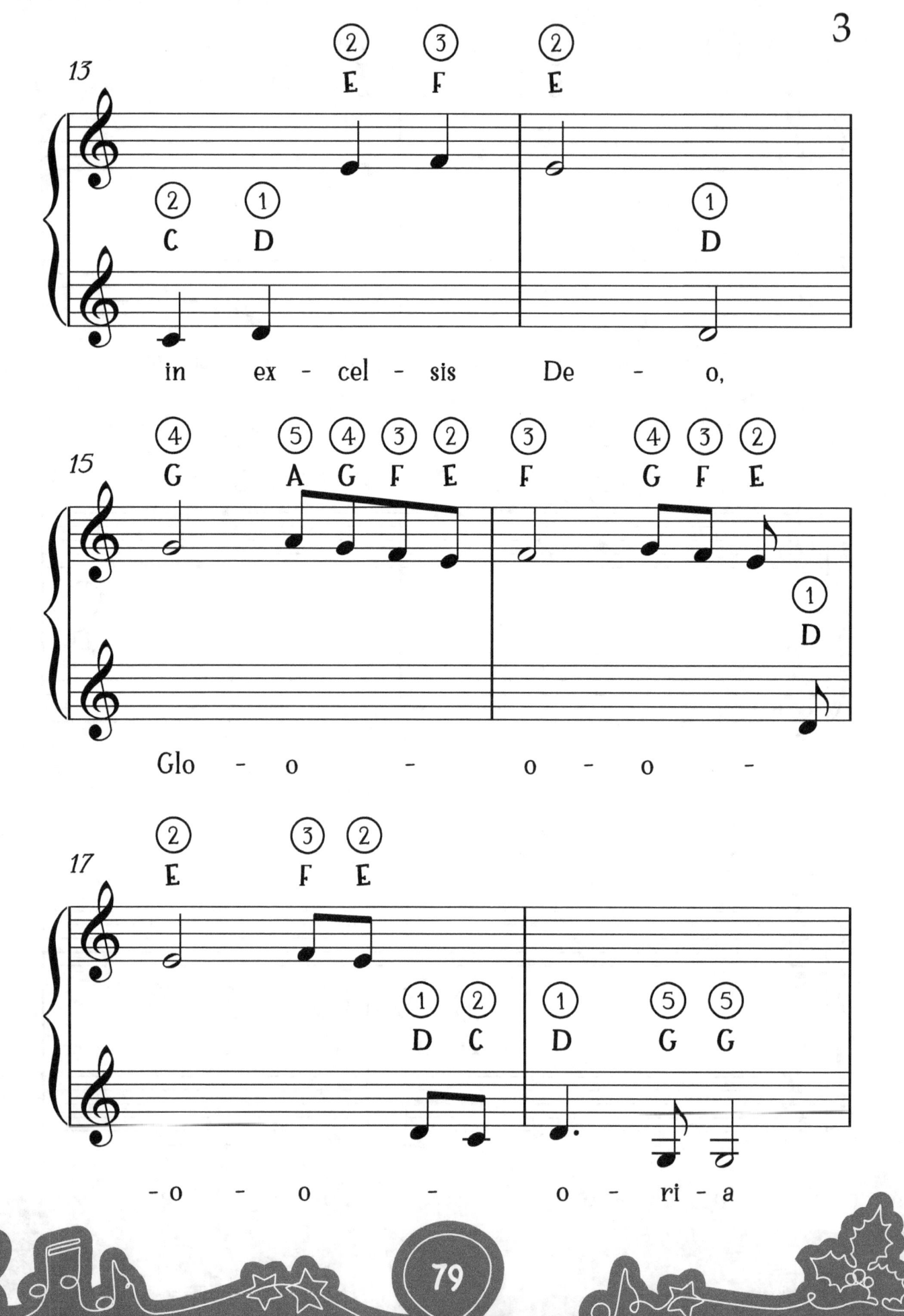

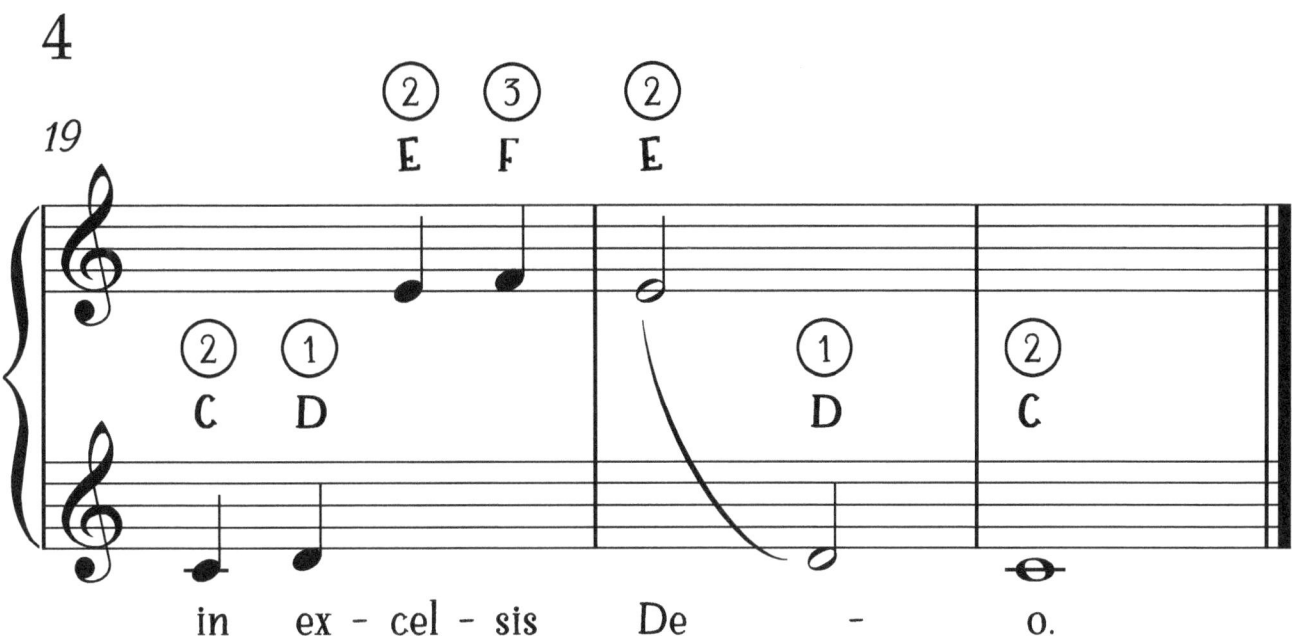

2. Shepherds, why this jubilee?
   Why your joyous strains prolong?
   What the gladsome tidings be
   Which inspire your heav'nly song?

Refrain

3. Come to Bethlehem and see
   Him whose birth the angels sing;
   Come, adore on bended knee
   Christ the Lord, the new-born King.

Refrain

4. See Him in a manger laid,
   Jesus, Lord of heav'n and earth!
   Mary, Joseph, lend your aid,
   Sing with us our Savior's birth.

Refrain

Away In a Manger

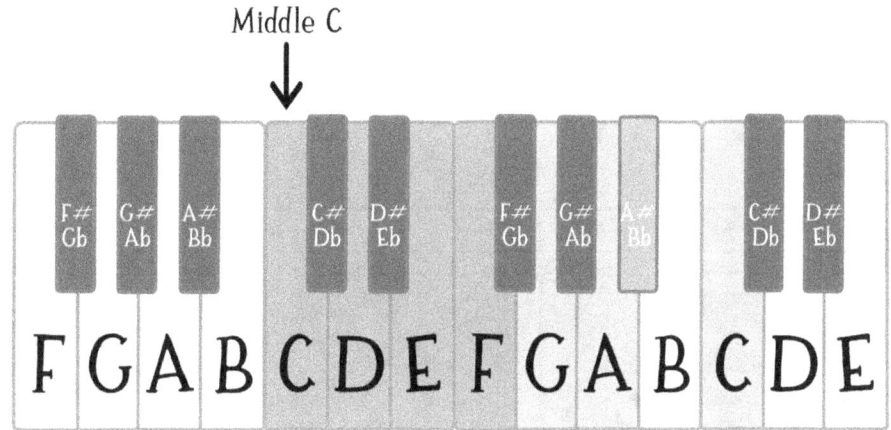

USEFUL TIP
at the end of
the song

AWAY IN A MANGER

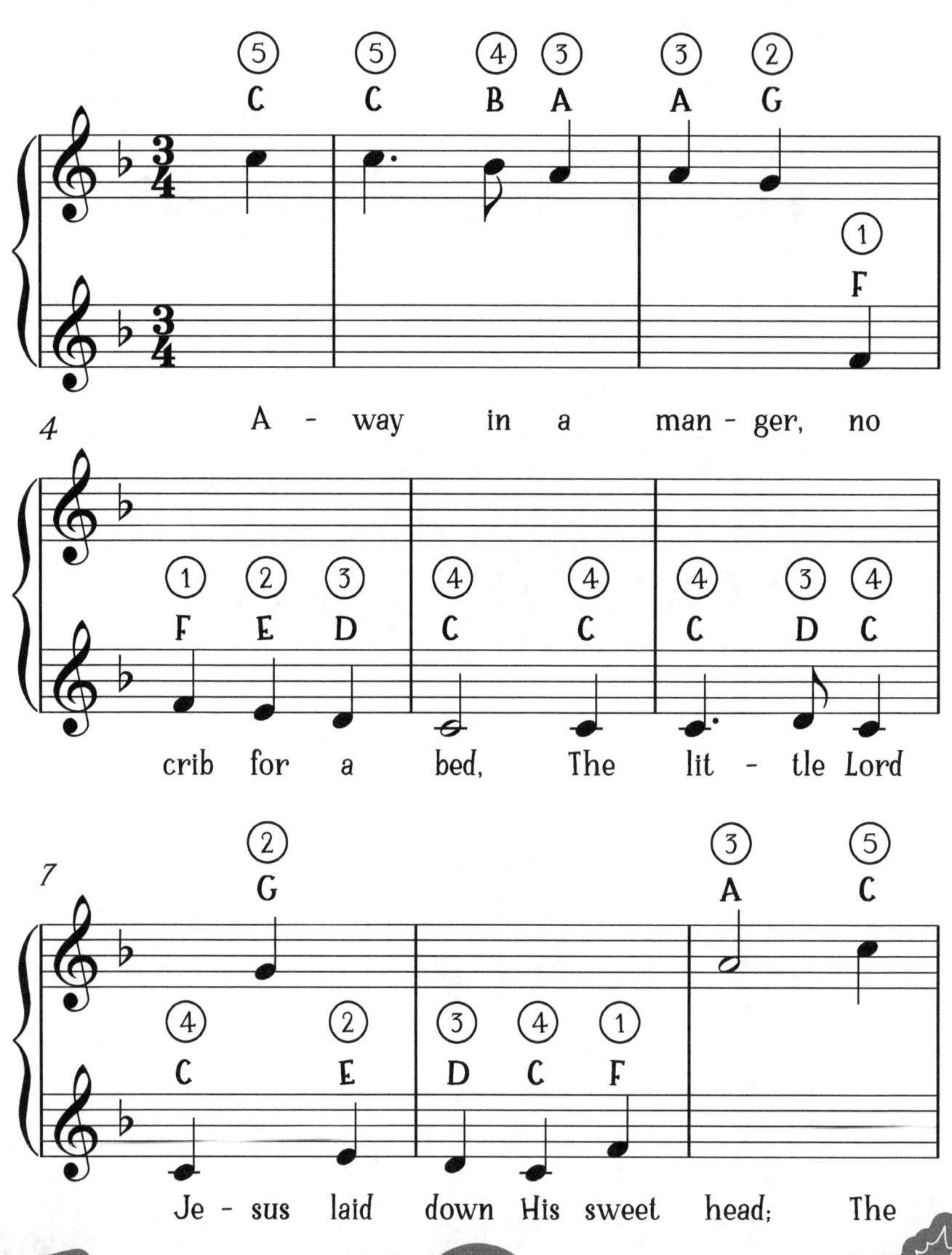

2. The cattle are lowing, the Baby awakes,
   But little Lord Jesus, no crying He makes.
   I love Thee, Lord Jesus, look down from the sky
   And stay by my side until morning is nigh.

3. Be near me, Lord Jesus; I ask Thee to stay
   Close by me forever, and love me, I pray.
   Bless all the dear children in Thy tender care,
   And fit us for heaven, to live with Thee there.

In this song, finger 1 of both hands will rest on F.

Silent Night

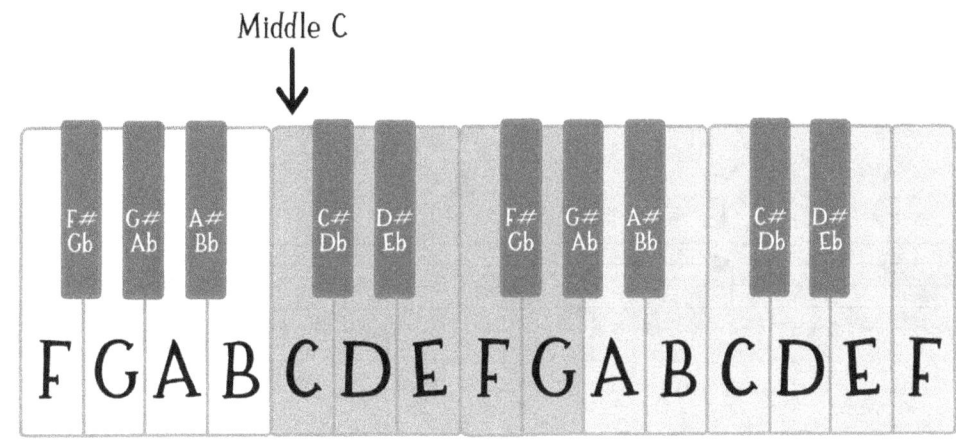

To make it more comfortable for playing, place your left hand so finger 1 will be on G. Finger 1 of your right hand will be on A.

SILENT NIGHT

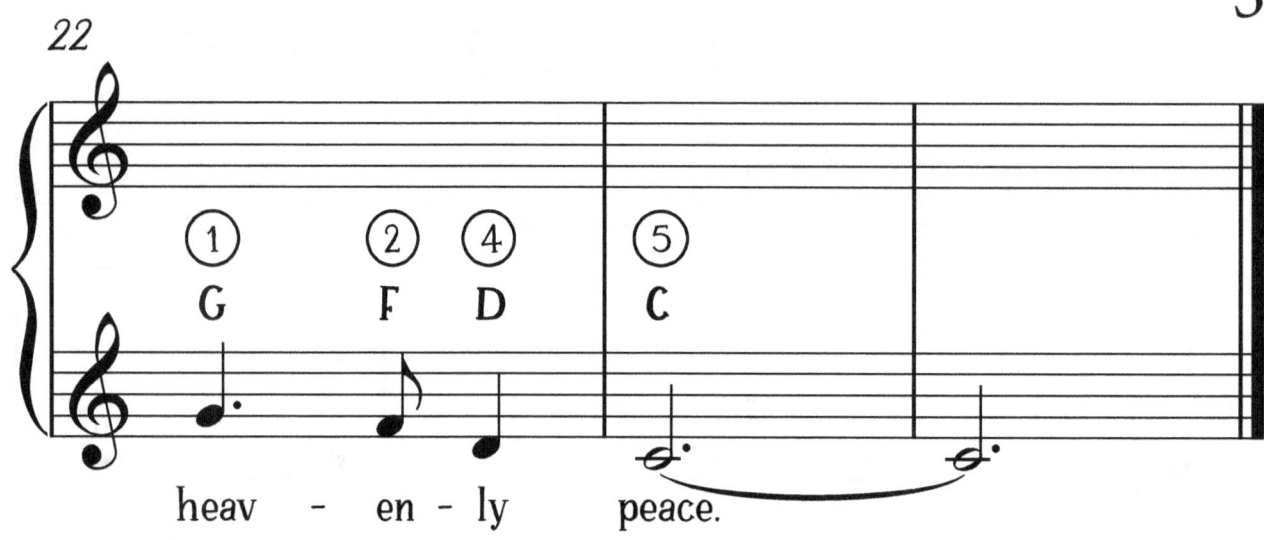

heav - en - ly peace.

2. Silent night! Holy night!
   Shepherds quake at the sight.
   Glories stream from heaven afar,
   Heav'nly hosts sing, "Alleluia!
   Christ the Savior is born!
   Christ the Savior is born!"

3. Silent night! Holy night!
   Son of God, love's pure light
   Radiant beams from Thy holy face
   With the dawn of redeeming grace,
   Jesus, Lord, at Thy birth!
   Jesus, Lord, at Thy birth!

4. Silent night! Holy night!
   Wondrous star, lend thy light;
   With the angels let us sing
   "Alleluia" to our King:
   "Christ the Savior is born!
   Christ the Savior is born."

O Come, O come, Emanuel

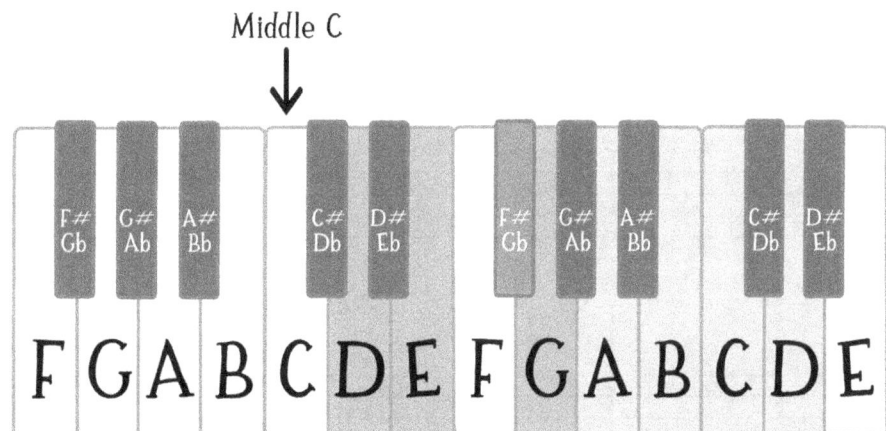

O COME, O COME, EMMANUEL

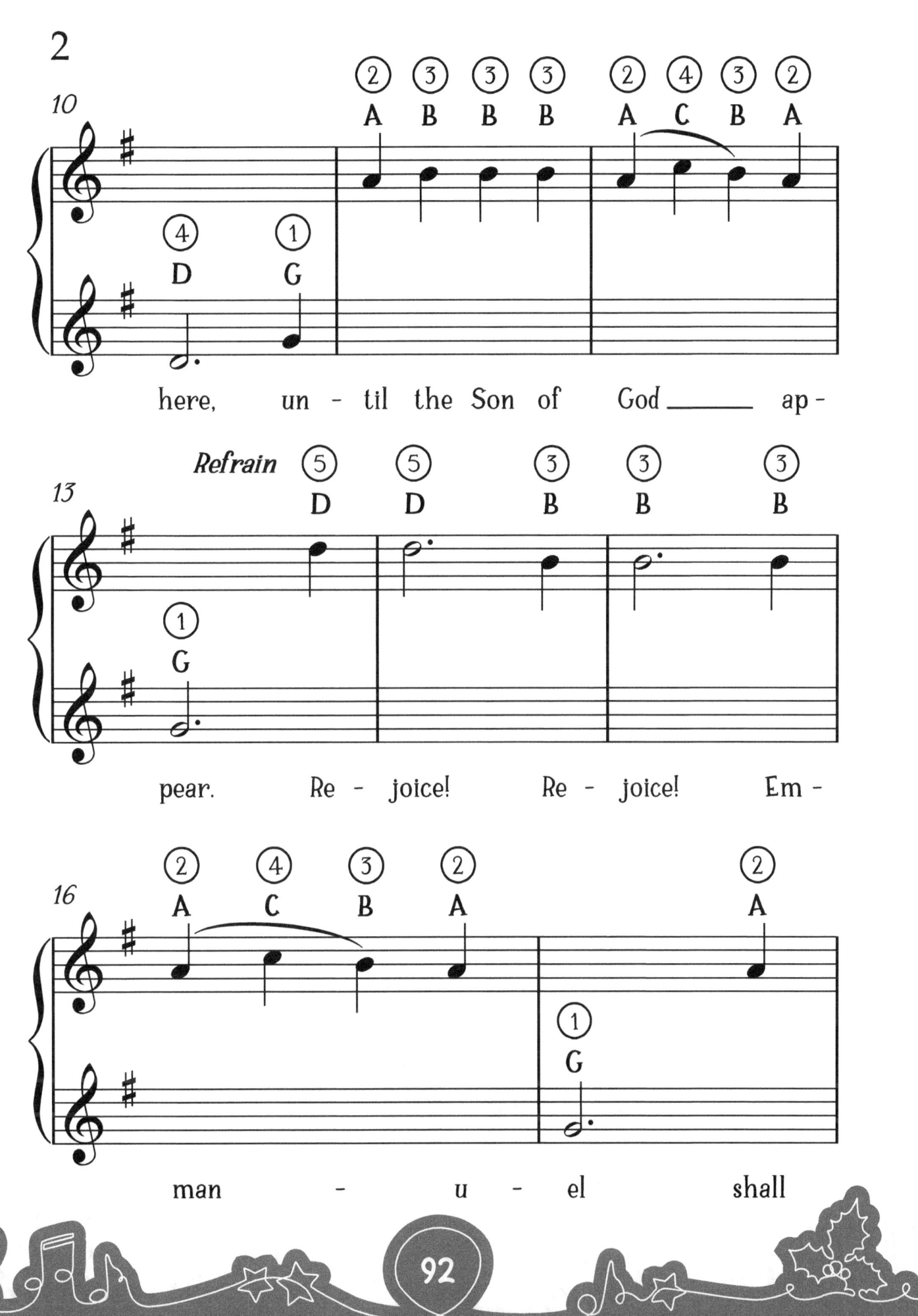

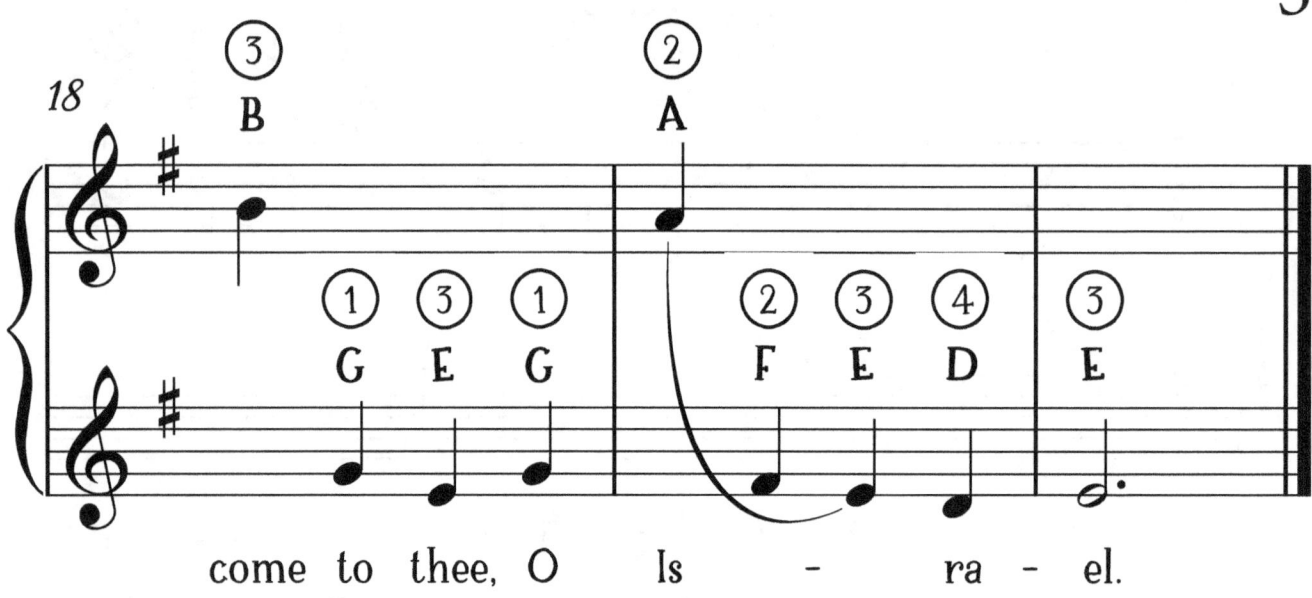

come to thee, O Is - ra - el.

2. O come, O Wisdom from on high,
   Who ordered all things mightily;
   To us the path of knowledge show
   And teach us in its ways to go.

Refrain

3. O come, O come, great Lord of might,
   Who to your tribes on Sinai's height
   In ancient times did give the law
   In cloud and majesty and awe.

Refrain

4. O come, O Branch of Jesse's stem,
   Unto your own and rescue them!
   From depths of hell your people save,
   And give them victory o'er the grave.

Refrain

5. O come, O Key of David, come
   And open wide our heavenly home.
   Make safe for us the heavenward road
   And bar the way to death's abode.

Refrain

6. O come, O Bright and Morning Star,
   And bring us comfort from afar!
   Dispel the shadows of the night
   And turn our darkness into light.

Refrain

7. O come, O King of nations, bind
   In one the hearts of all mankind.
   Bid all our sad divisions cease
   And be yourself our King of Peace. Refrain

Chapter 4

O Little Town of Bethlehem

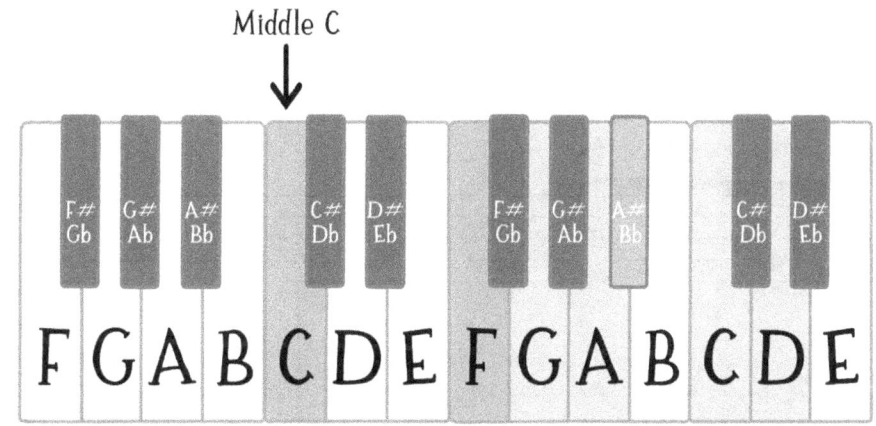

Place both thumbs on G, and the rest of the notes will be right under your fingers.

O LITTLE TOWN OF BETHLEHEM

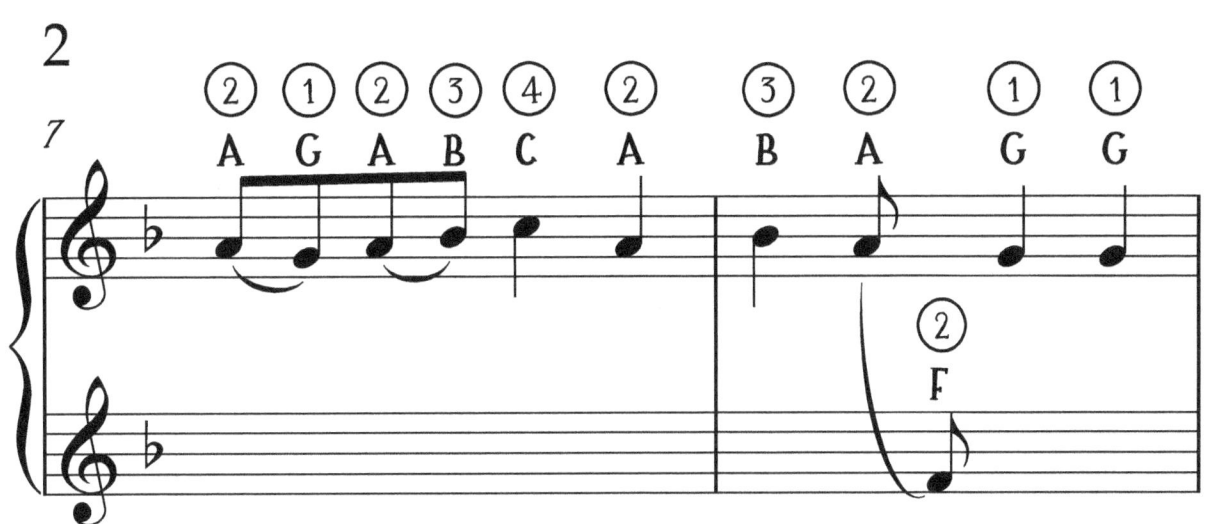
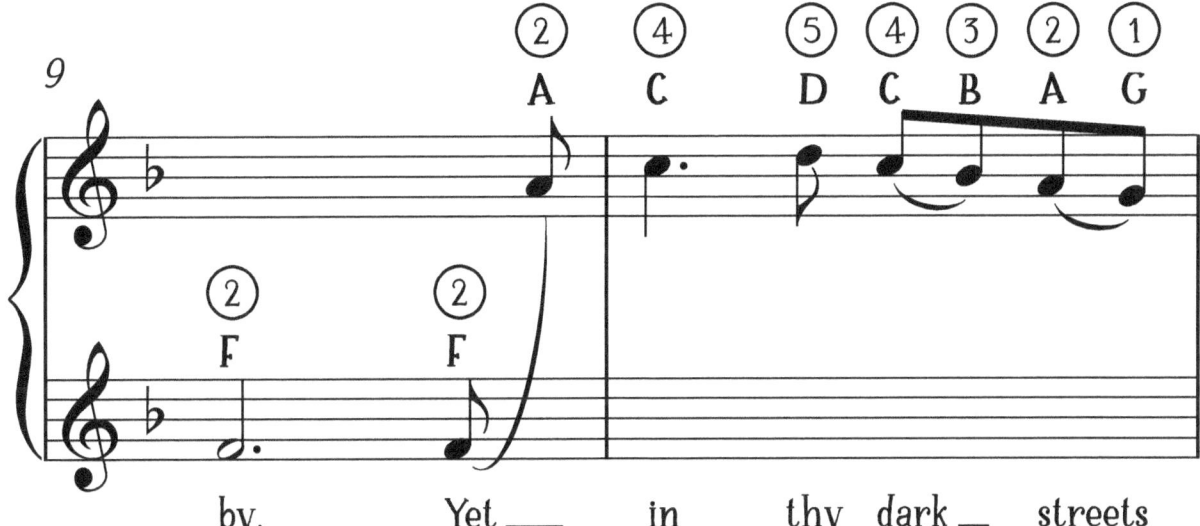
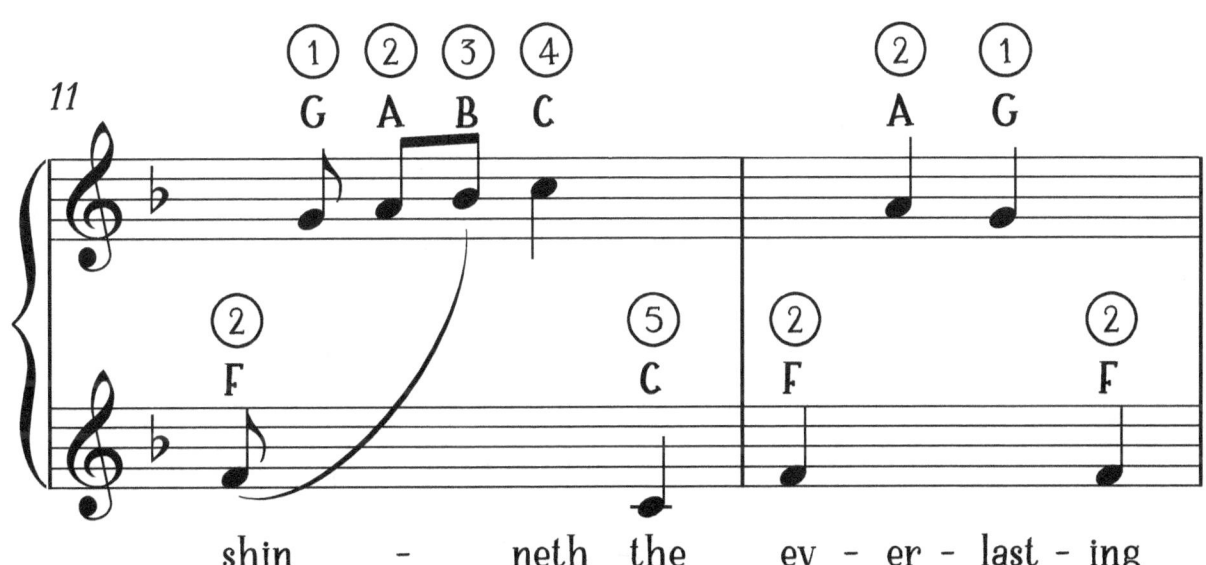

2. For Christ is born of Mary;
   And, gathered all above,
   While mortals sleep, the angels keep
   Their watch of wond'ring love.
   O morning stars, together
   Proclaim the holy birth,
   And praises sing to God the King,
   And peace to men on earth.

3. How silently, how silently,
   The wondrous gift is giv'n!
   So God imparts to human hearts
   The blessings of His heav'n.
   No ear may hear His coming,
   But in this world of sin,
   Where meek souls will receive Him still,
   The dear Christ enters in.

4. O holy Child of Bethlehem,
   Descend to us, we pray;
   Cast out our sin and enter in;
   Be born in us today.
   We hear the Christmas angels,
   The great glad tidings tell;
   O come to us, abide with us,
   Our Lord Emmanuel!

Once in Royal David's City

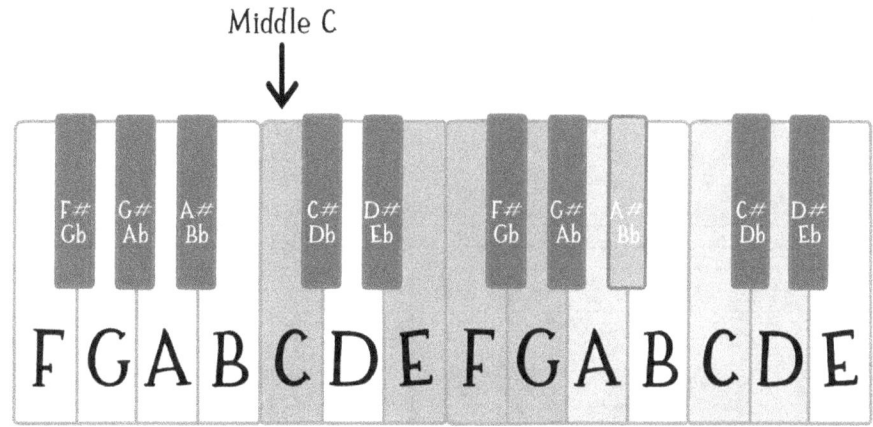

USEFUL TIP at the end of the song

ONCE IN ROYAL DAVID'S CITY

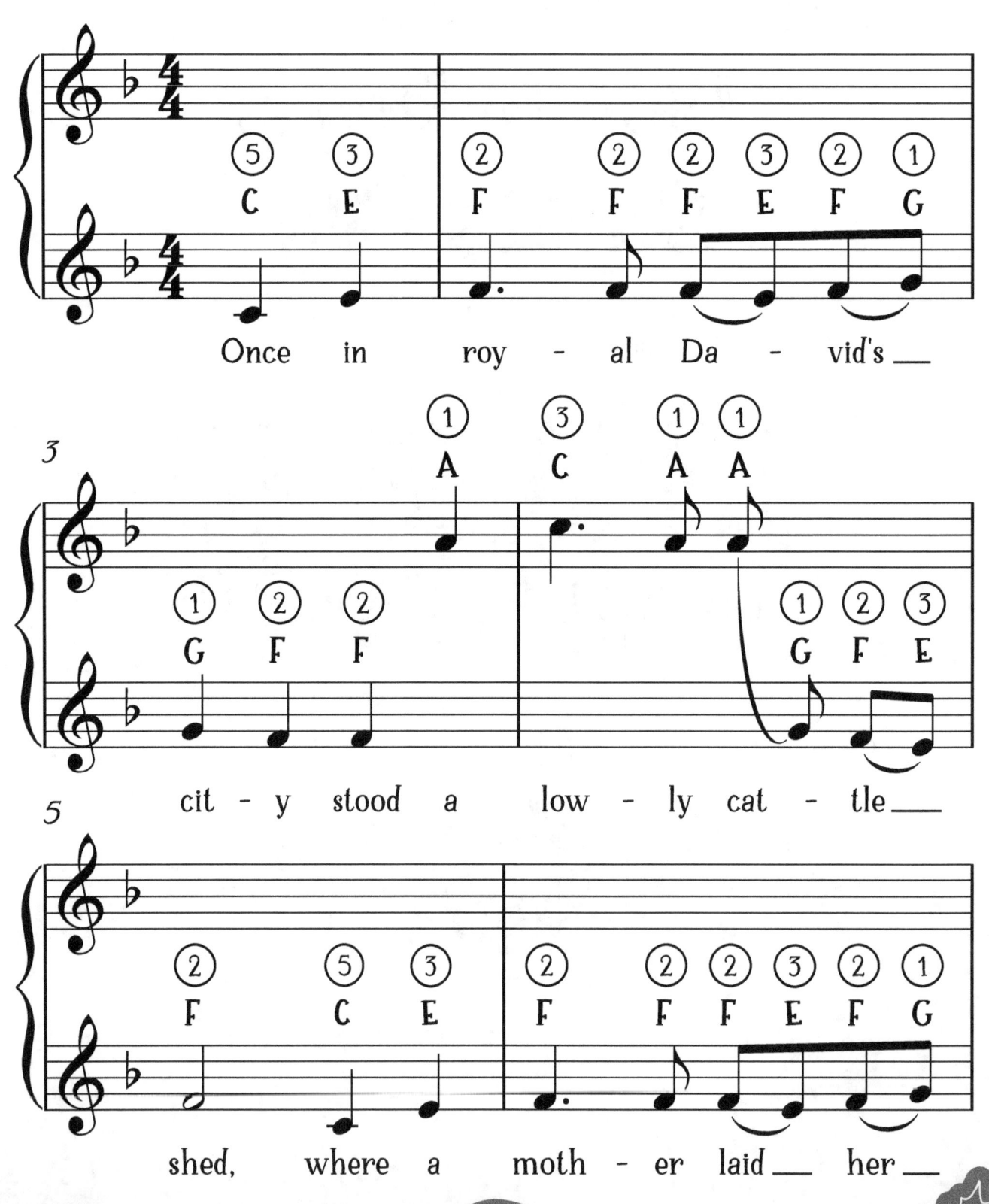

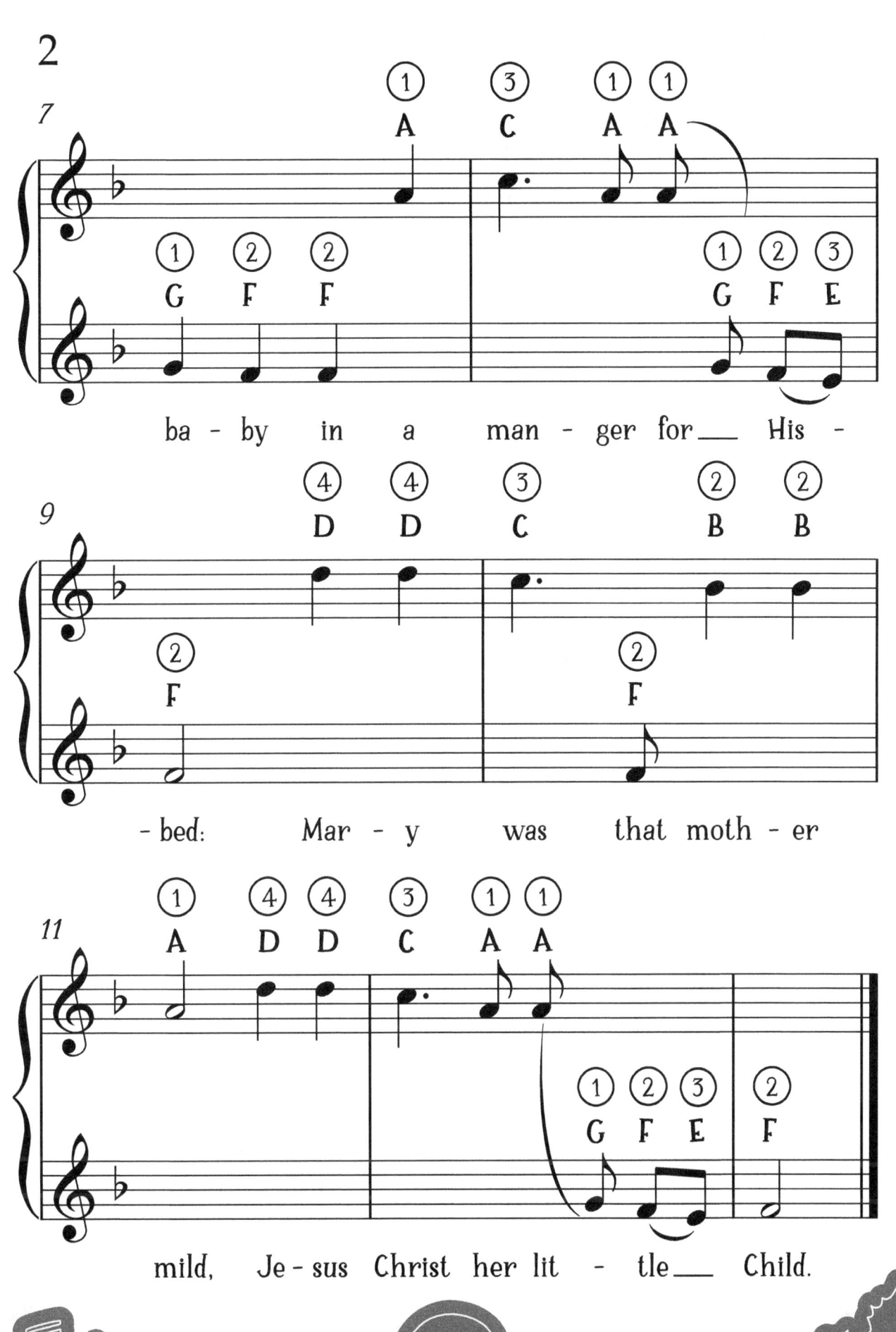

2. He came down to earth from heaven
   Who is God and Lord of all,
   And His shelter was a stable,
   And His cradle was a stall:
   With the poor, and meek, and lowly,
   Lived on earth our Savior holy.

3. And our eyes at last shall see Him,
   Through His own redeeming love;
   For that Child so dear and gentle
   Is our Lord in heav'n above,
   And He leads His children on
   To the place where He is gone.

4. Not in that poor lowly stable,
   With the oxen standing by,
   We shall see Him, but in heaven,
   Set at God's right hand on high;
   When like stars His children crowned
   All in white shall wait around.

Place your left hand finger 1 on G and right hand finger 1 on A.

Hark, the Herald Angels Sing

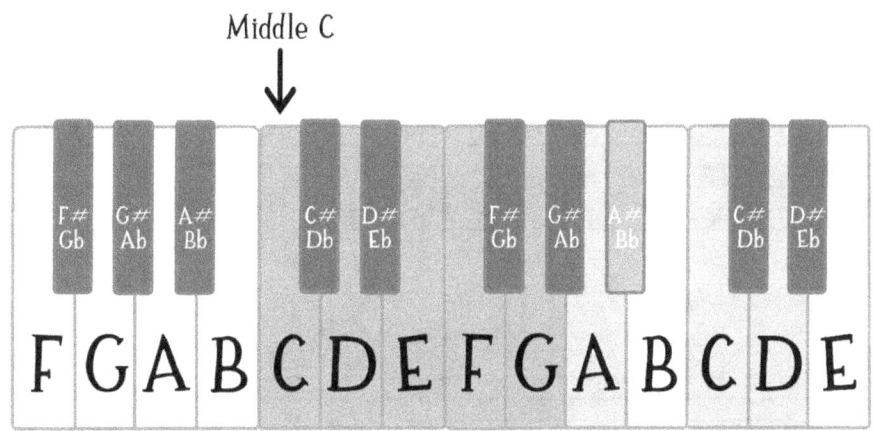

HARK! THE HERALD ANGELS SING

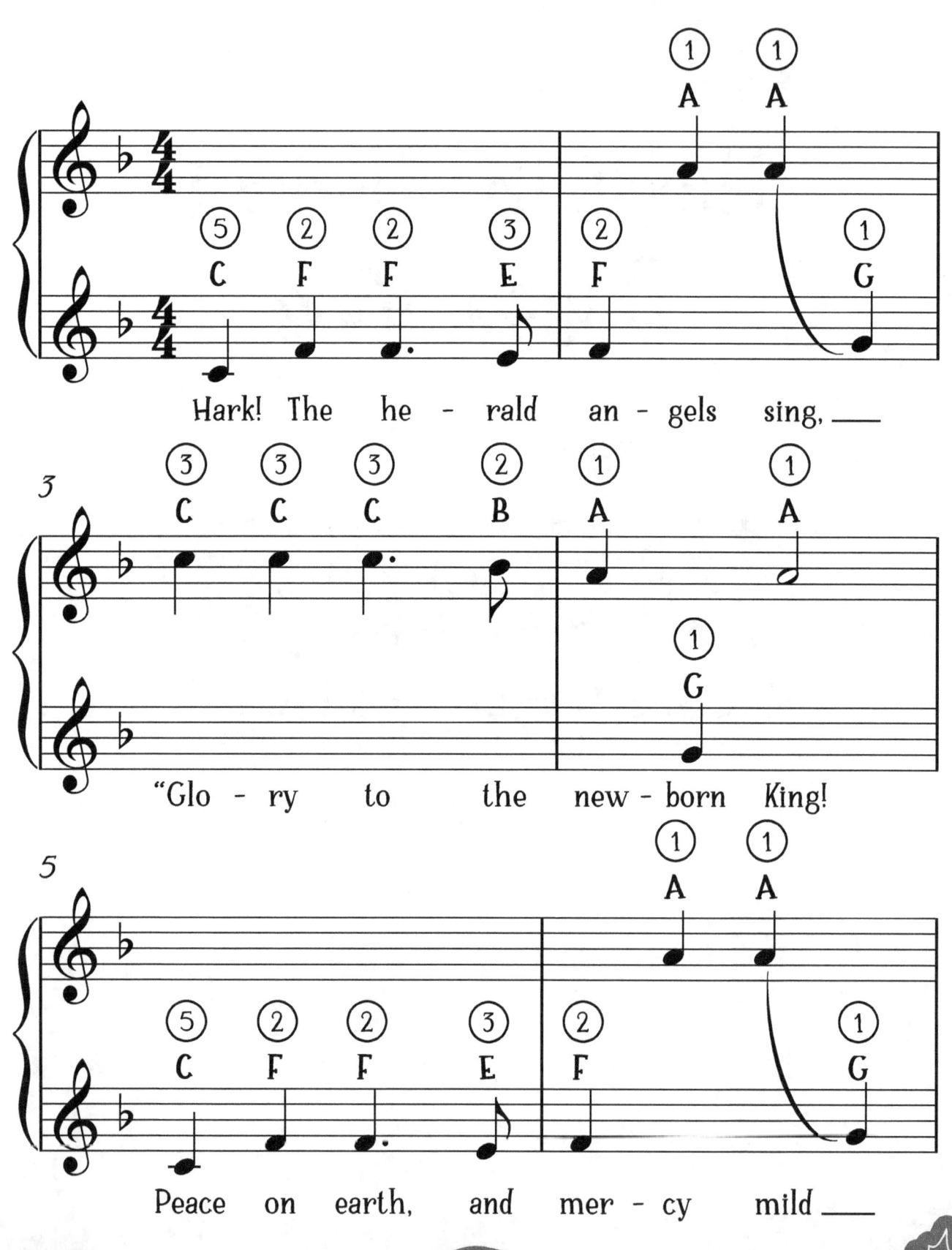

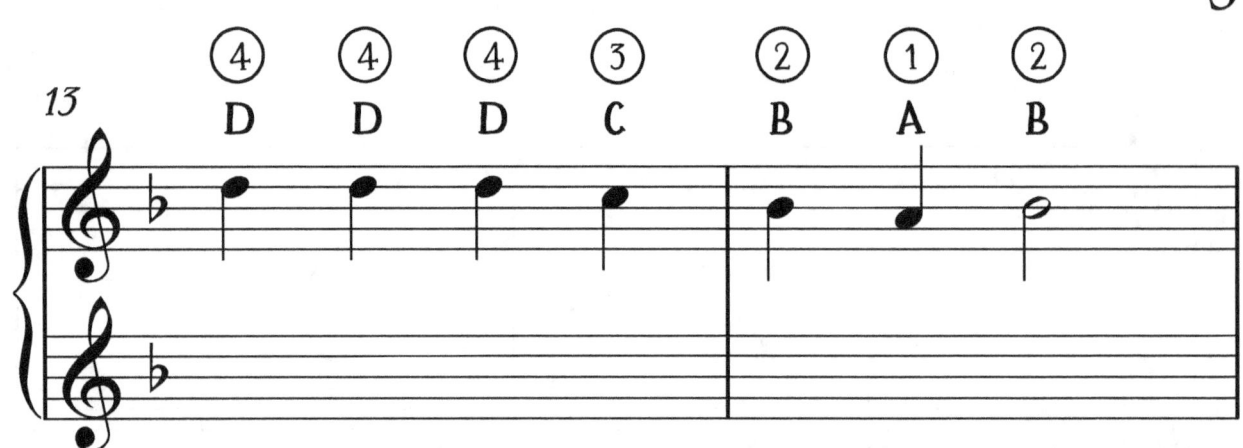
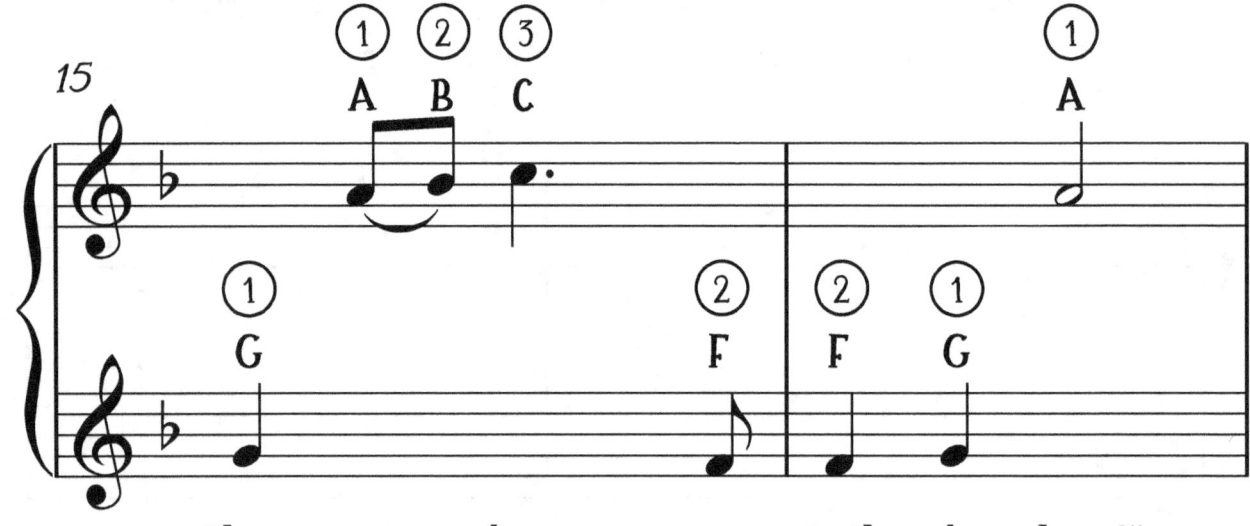
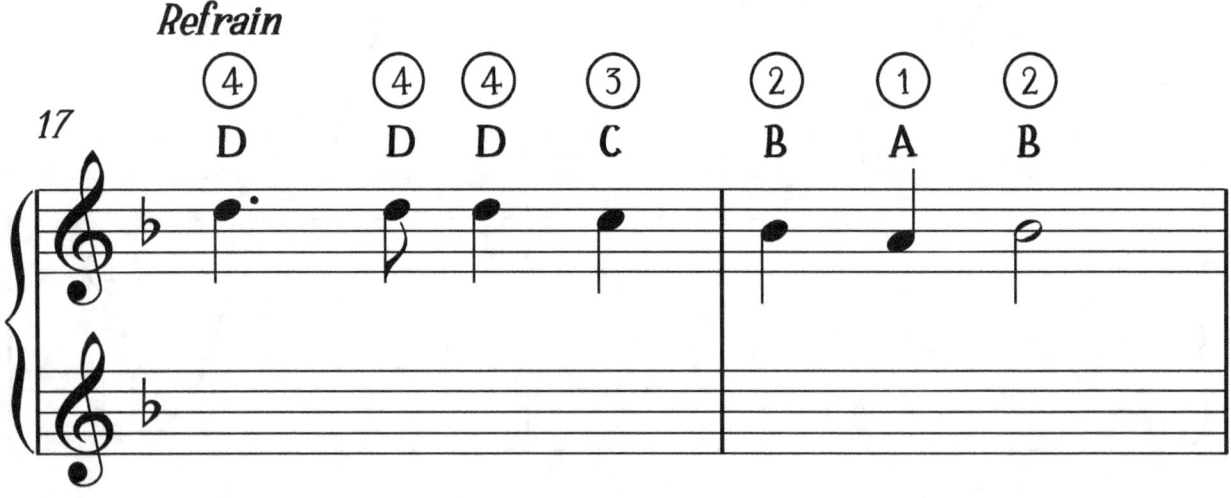

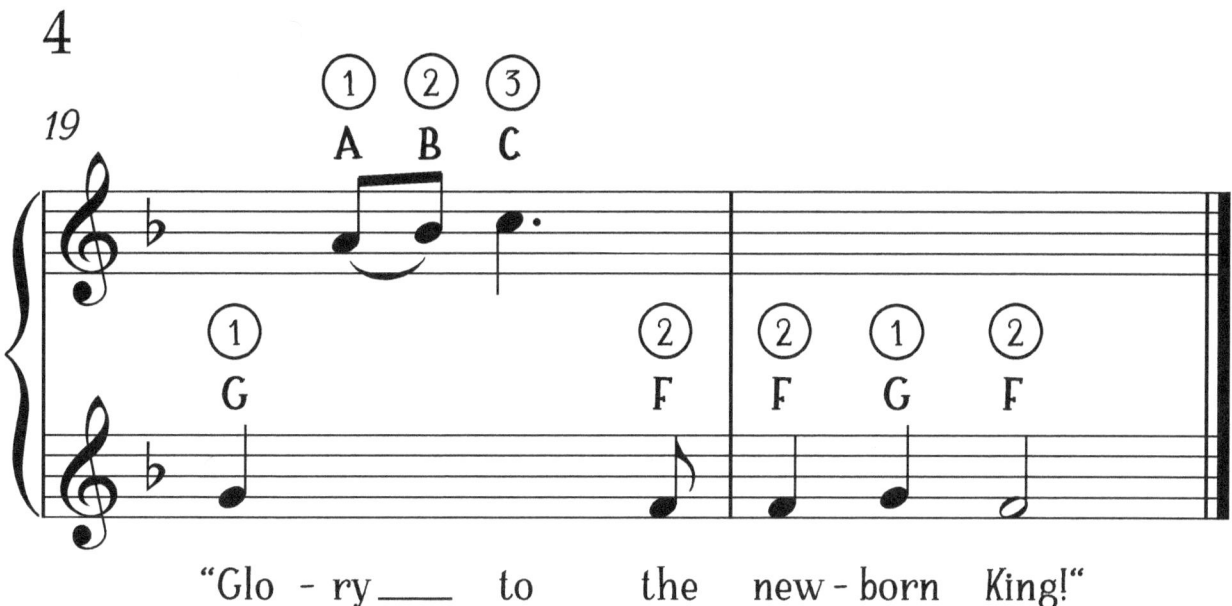

"Glo - ry ___ to the new-born King!"

2. Christ by highest heav'n adored;
   Christ, the everlating Lord!
   Late in time behold Him come,
   Offspring of the Virgin's womb:
   Veiled in flesh the God-head see;
   Hail th'incarnate Deity;
   Pleased as man with men to dwell,
   Jesus, Our Emmanuel!

Refrain

3. Hail the heav'n-born Prince of Peace!
   Hail the Son of Righteousness!
   Light and lift to all He brings,
   Ris'n with healing in His wings.
   Mild He lays His glory by,
   Born that men no more may die,
   Born to raise the sons of earth,
   Born to give them second birth.

Refrain

Auld Lang Syne

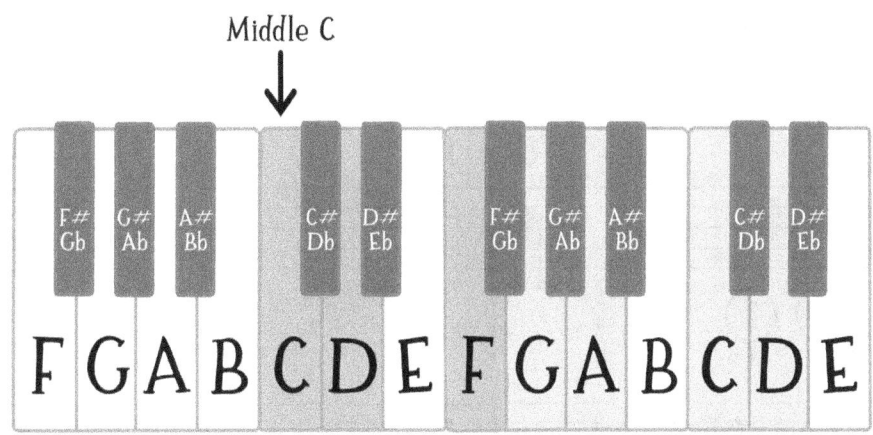

Interesting fact

"Auld lang syne" (sounds like: aald lang zine) is a phrase from Gaelic Scottish. It means "for old times' sake."

AULD LANG SYNE*

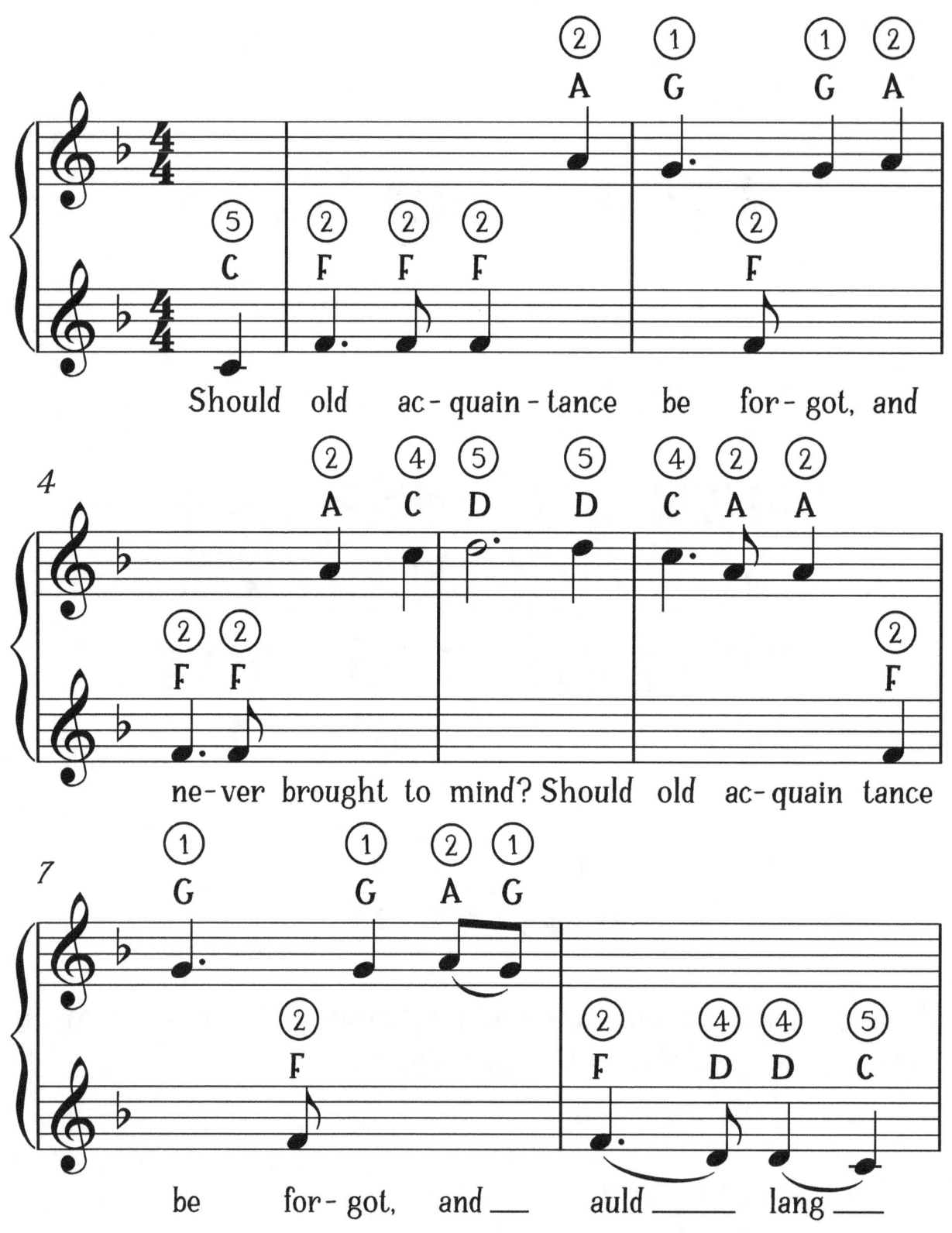

* "For Old Time's Sake" (from Gaelic Scotish)

Jingle Bells

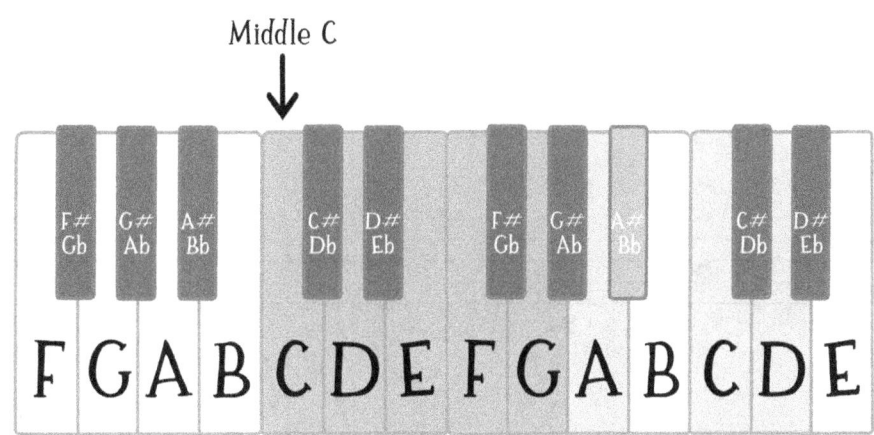

JINGLE BELLS

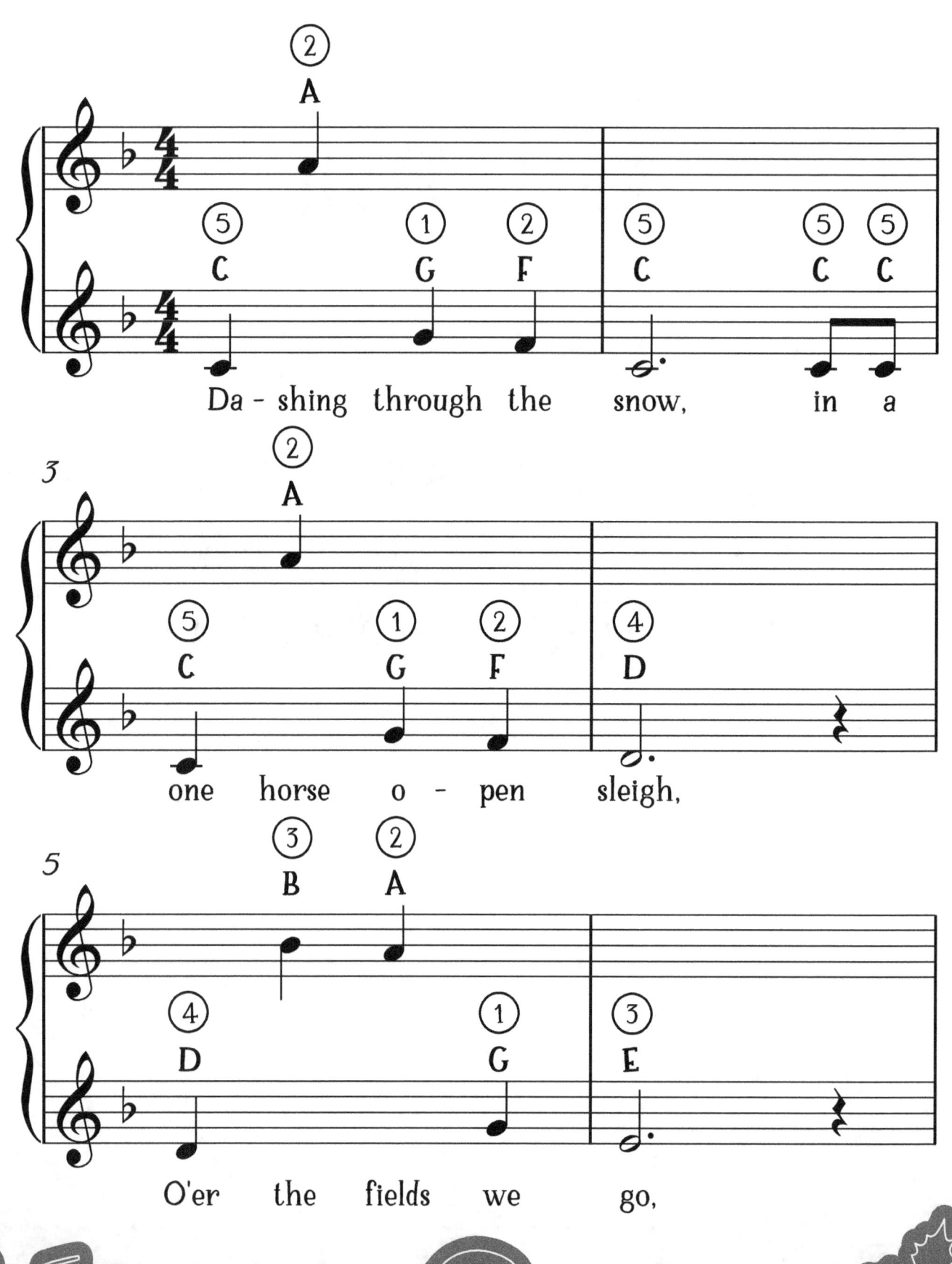

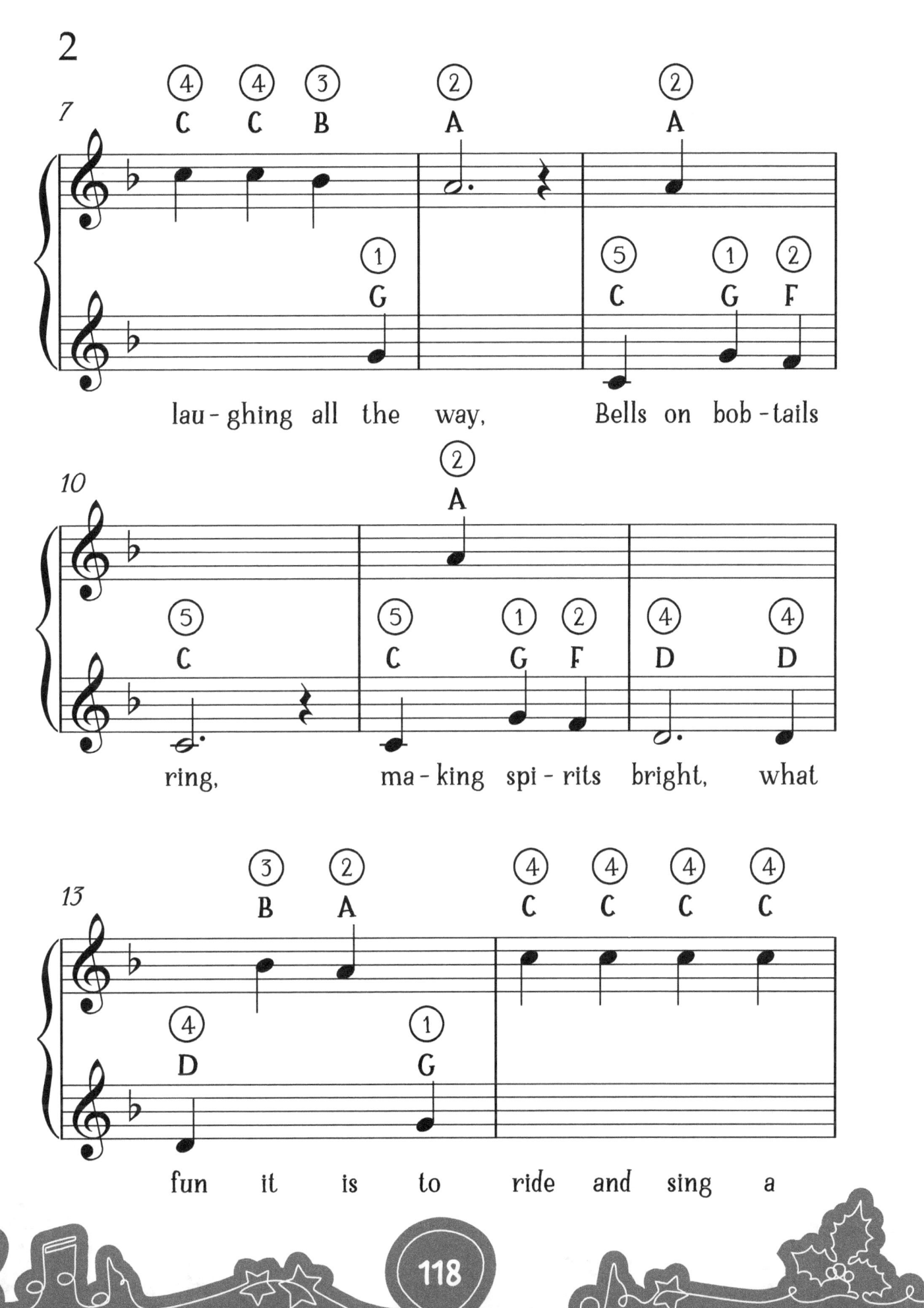

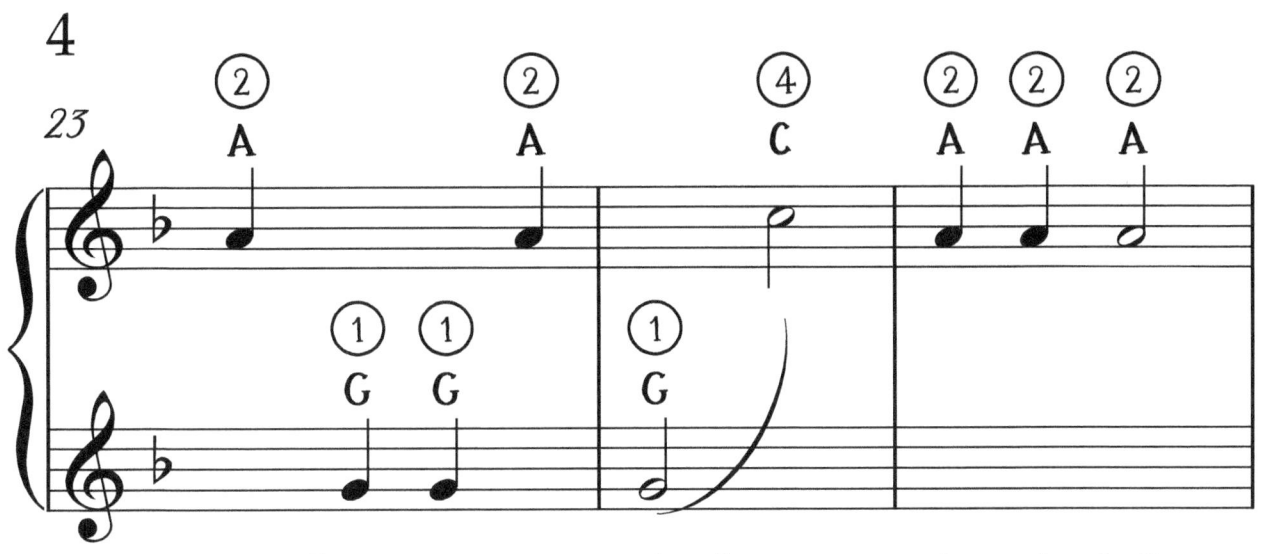
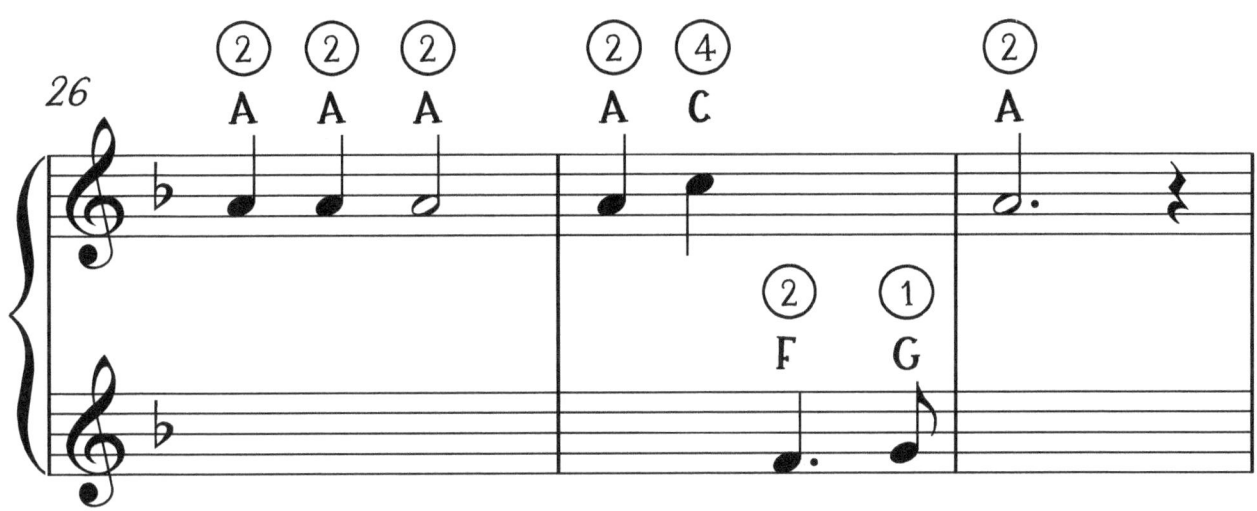
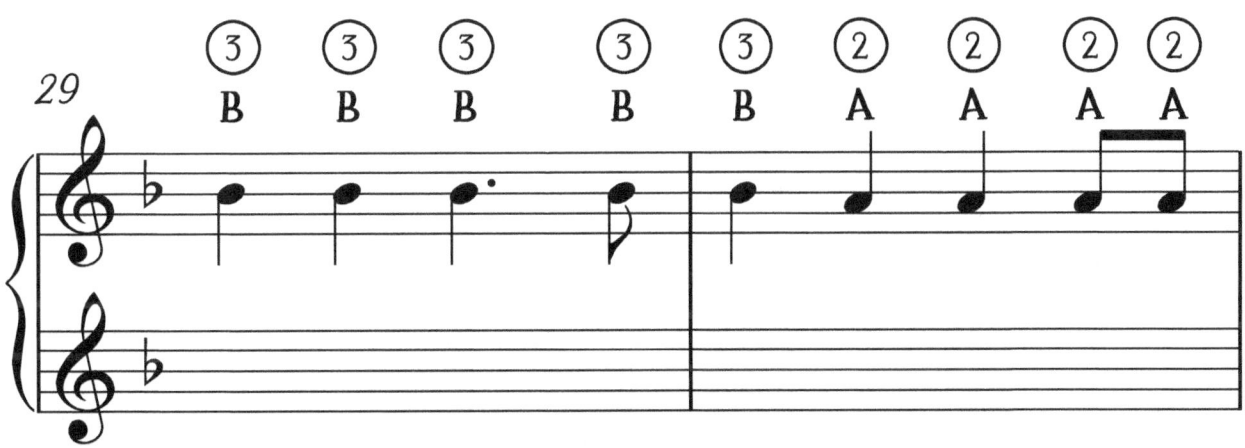

one - horse o - pen sleigh.

2. A day or two ago
   I thought I'd take a ride
   And soon, Miss Fanny Bright
   Was seated by my side,
   The horse was lean and lank
   Misfortune seemed his lot
   He got into a drifted bank
   And then we got upsot.

Chorus

3. A day or two ago,
   The story I must tell
   I went out on the snow,
   And on my back I fell;
   A gent was riding by
   In a one-horse open sleigh,
   He laughed as there I sprawling lie,
   But quickly drove away.

Chorus

4. Now the ground is white
   Go it while you're young,
   Take the girls tonight
   And sing this sleighing song;
   Just get a bobtailed bay
   Two forty as his speed
   Hitch him to an open sleigh
   And crack! you'll take the lead.

Chorus

O Christmas Tree

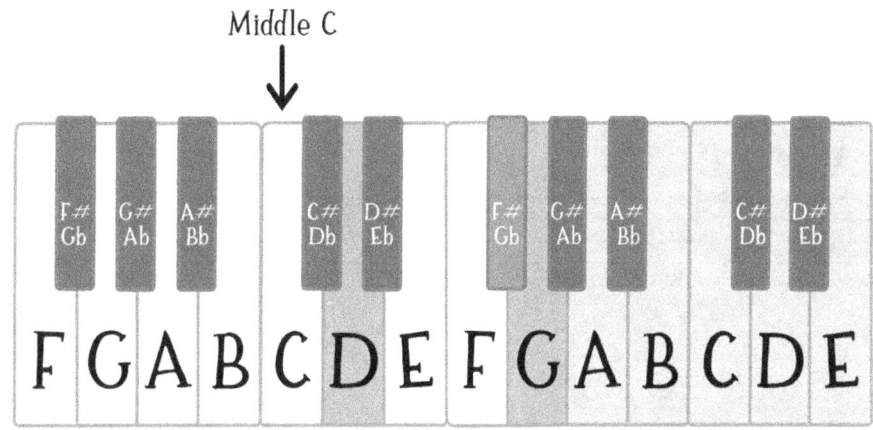

USEFUL TIP at the end of the song

O CHRISTMAS TREE

2

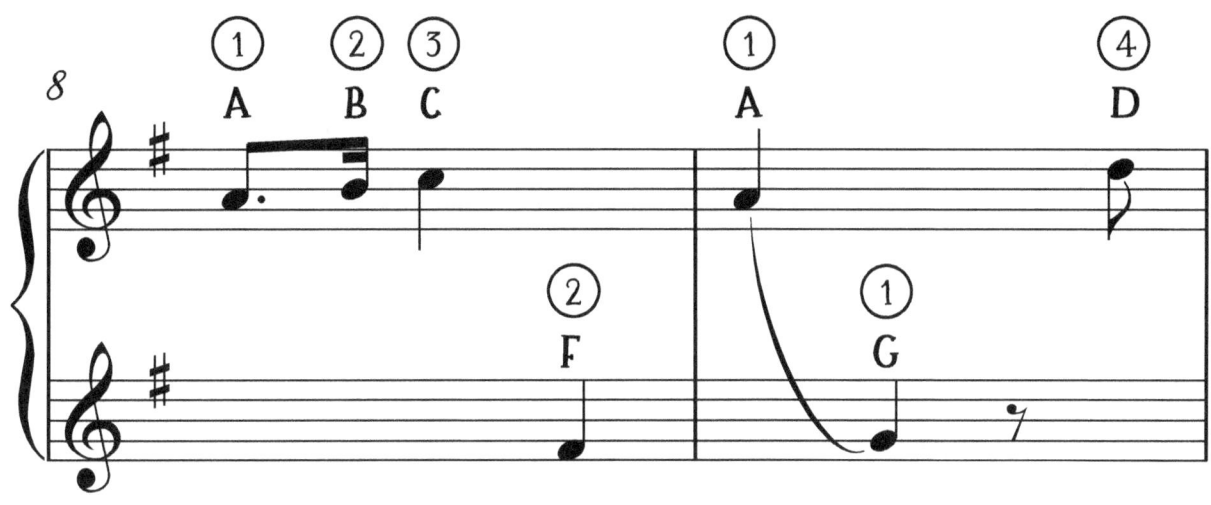
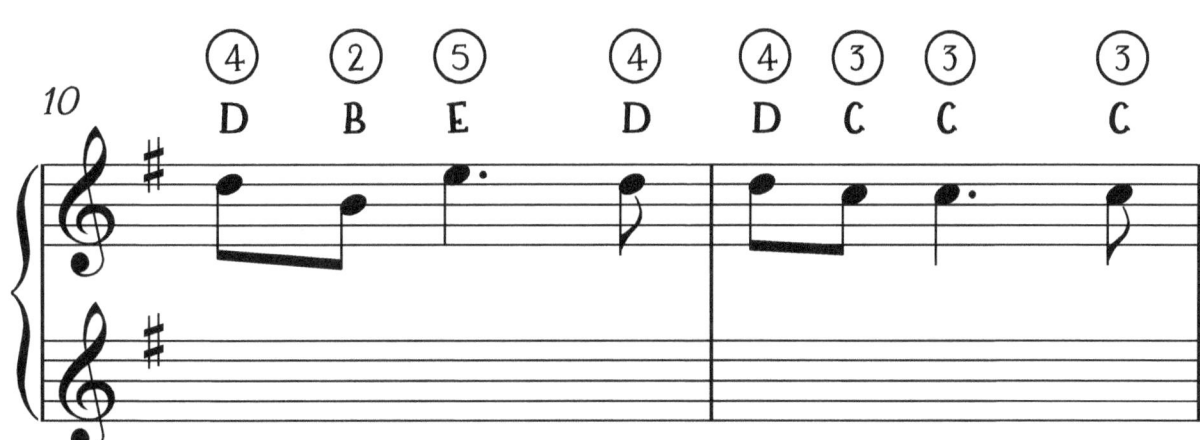
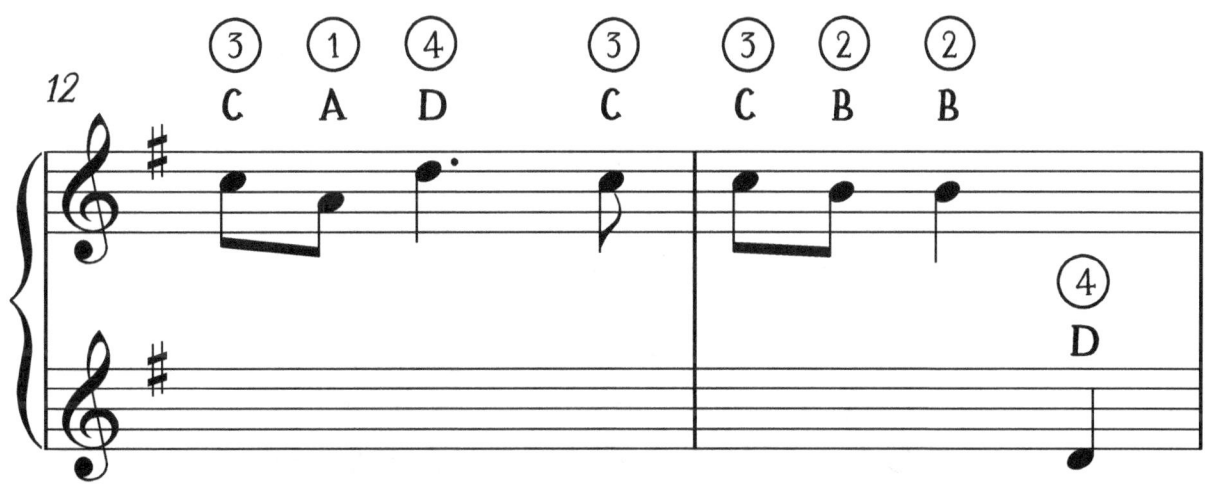

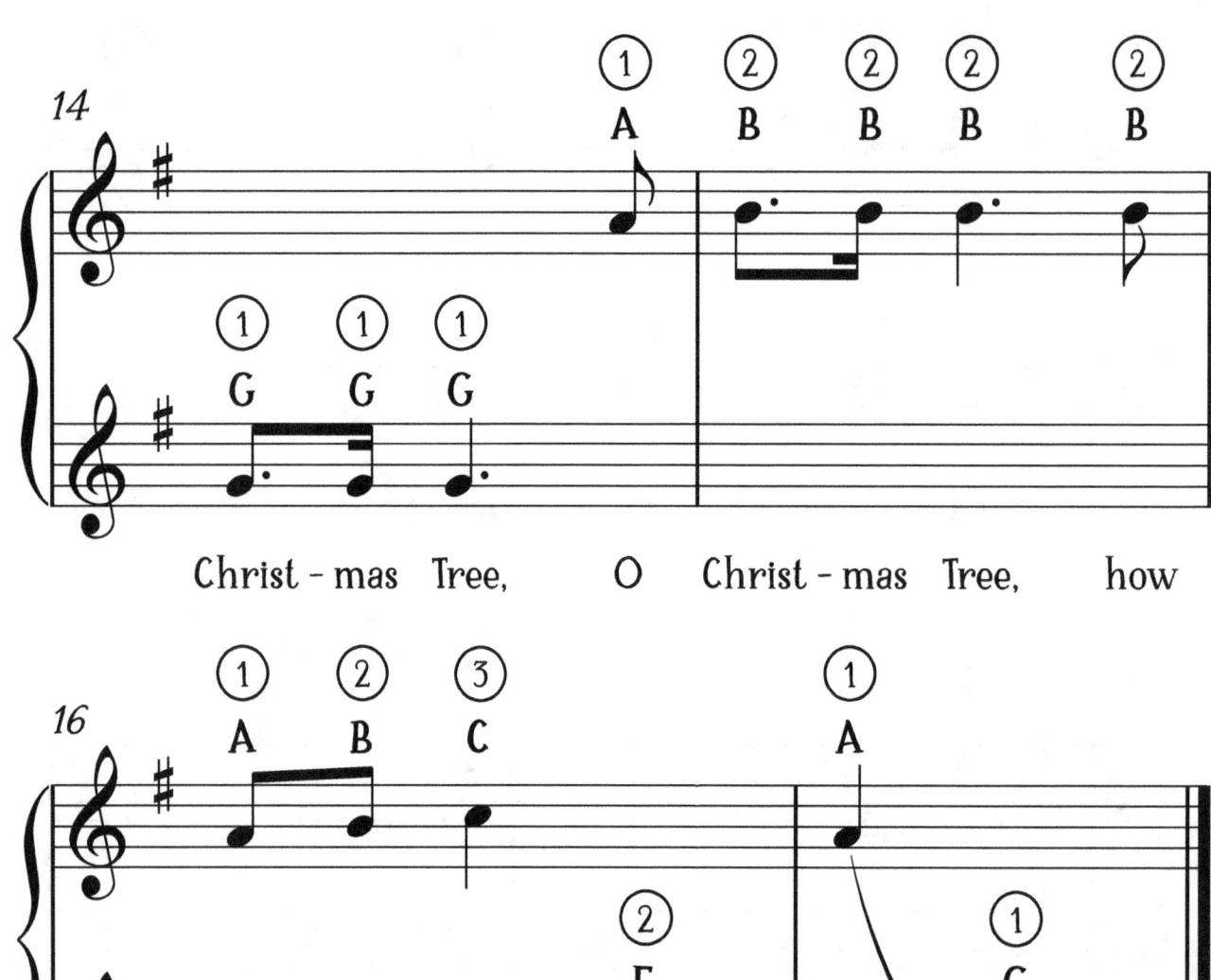

2. O Christmas Tree, O Christmas Tree,
   Thy leaves teach me a lesson;
   O Christmas Tree, O Christmas Tree,
   Thy leaves teach me a lesson;
   For they give hope and constancy
   Give strength and courage unto me;
   O Christmas Tree, O Christmas Tree,
   Thy leaves teach me a lesson;

Dotted rhythm with eighth and sixteenths

Do you remember how to play a dotted quarter note? This song has dotted quarter notes-as well as dotted eighth and sixteenth notes. Check the tip for song Coventry, Carol if you need a reminder of how dotted rhythms work.

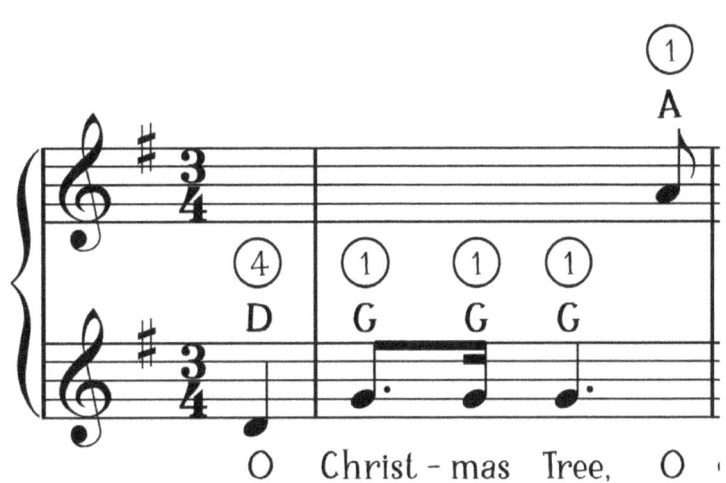

O Come All Ye Faithful

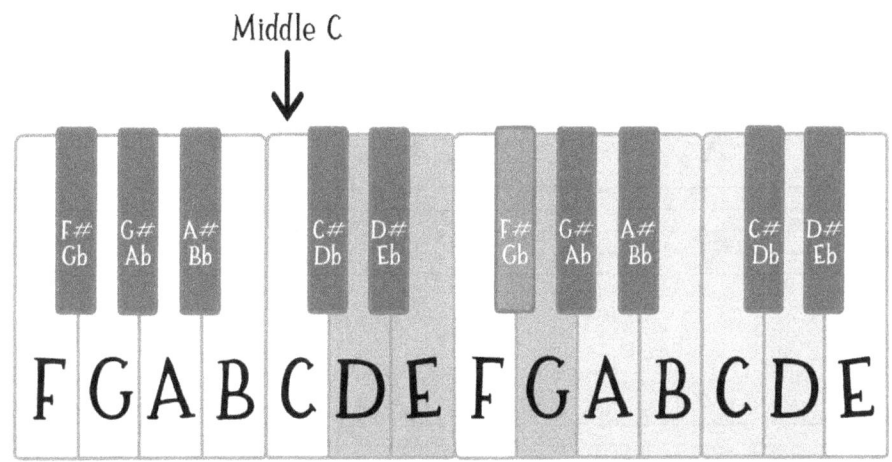

38. O COME, ALL YE FAITHFUL

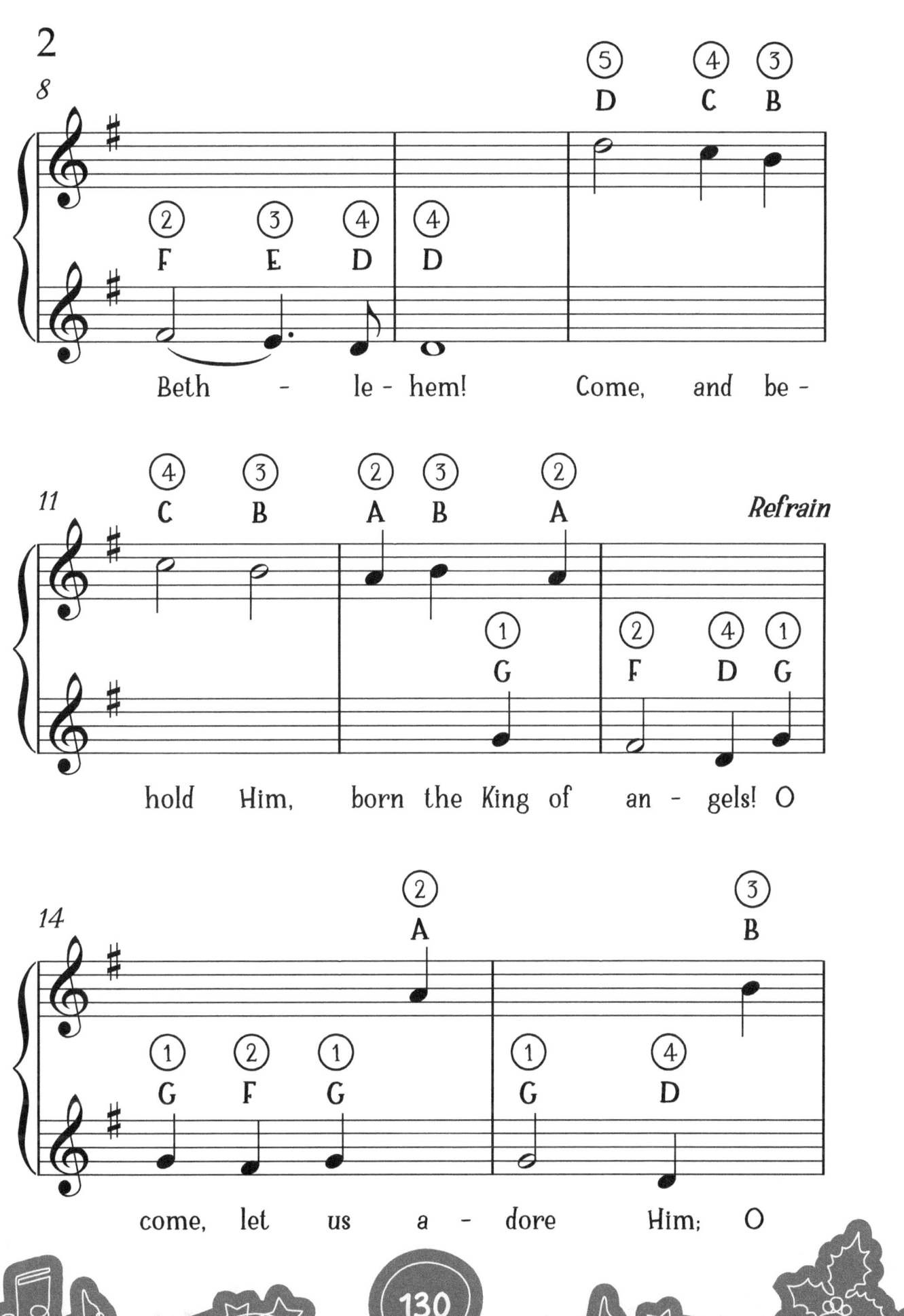

16
3 2 3 4 3 2 3
B A B C B A B
come, let us a - dore Him; O
18
4 3 2 4
C B A C
1 2 1
G F G
come, let us a - dore Him,
20
3 2
B A
1 1
G G
Christ, the Lord!

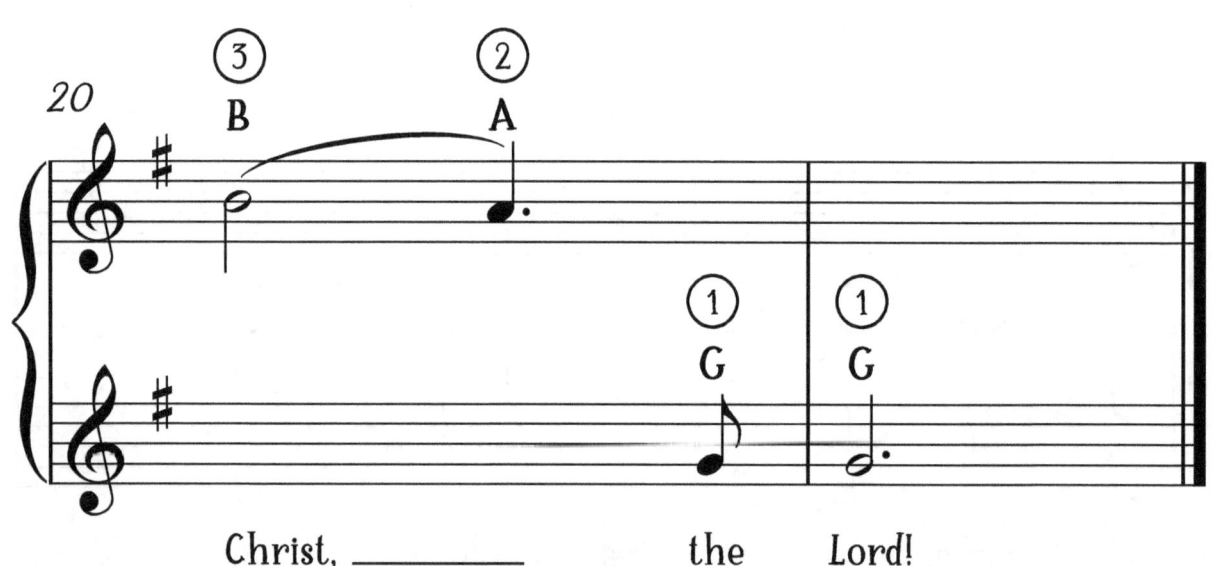

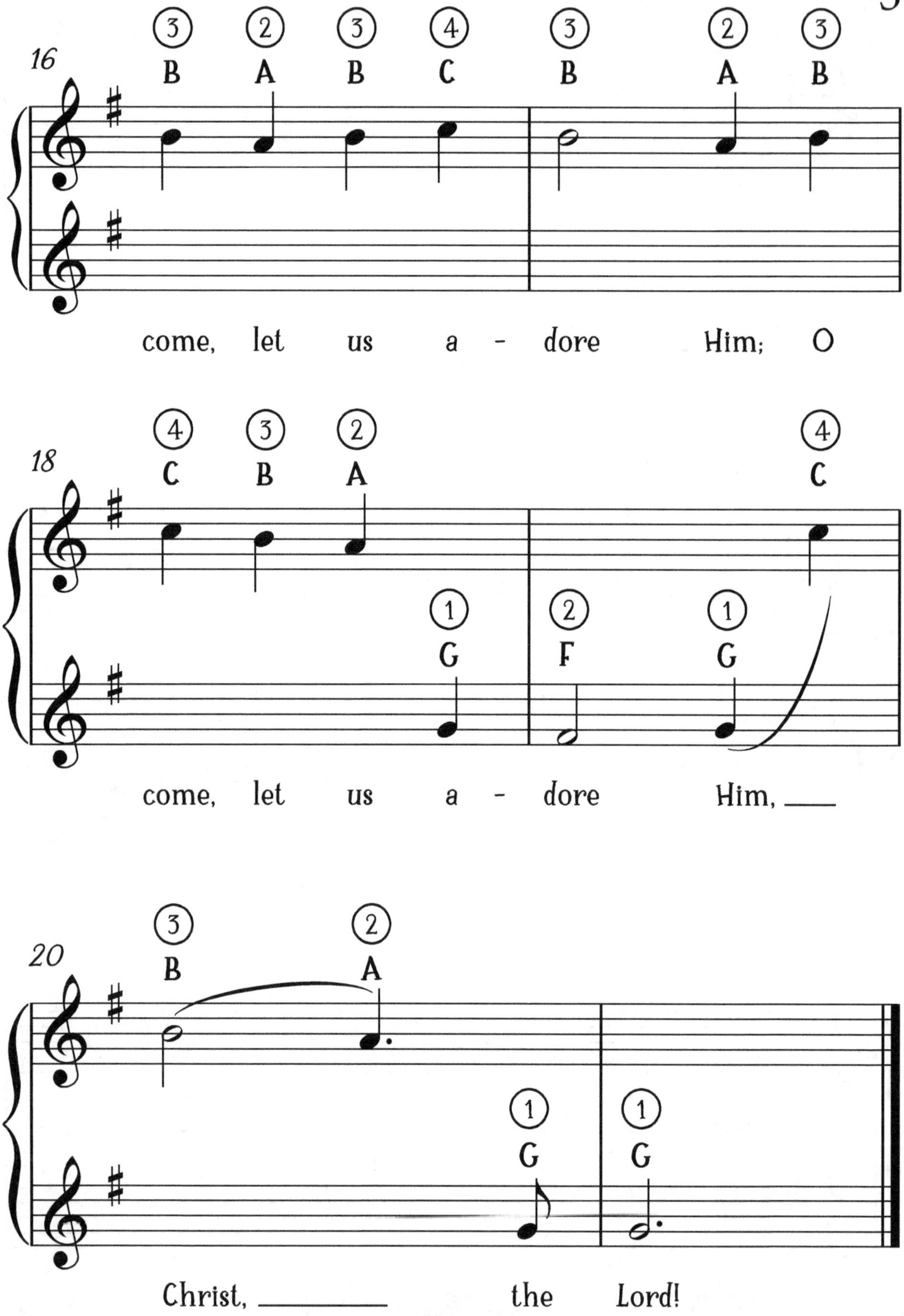

2. God of God, Light of Light,
   Lo, He abhors not the virgin's womb;
   Very God, begotten not created;

Refrain

3. Sing, choirs of angels; sing in exultation;
   Sing, all ye citizens of heav'n above!
   Glory to God, all glory in the highest!

Refrain

4. Yea, Lord, we greet Thee, born this happy morning;
   Jesus, to Thee be all glory giv'n!
   Word of the Father, now in flesh appearing!

Refrain

Chapter 5

Here We Come A-Wassailing

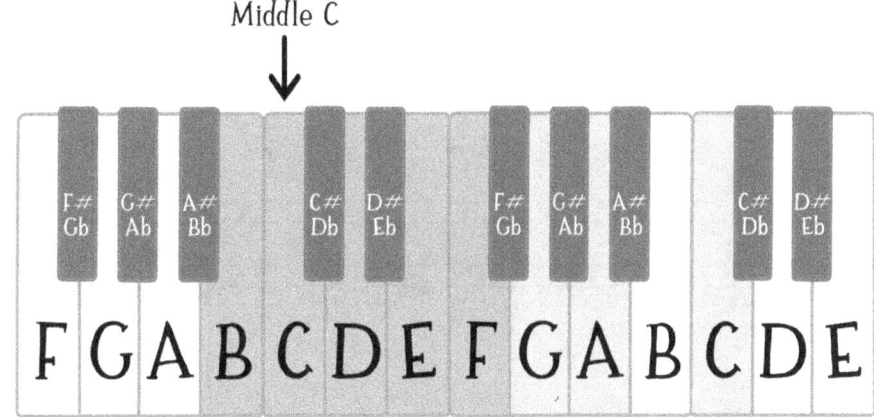

USEFUL TIP at the end of the song

HERE WE COME A-WASSAILING

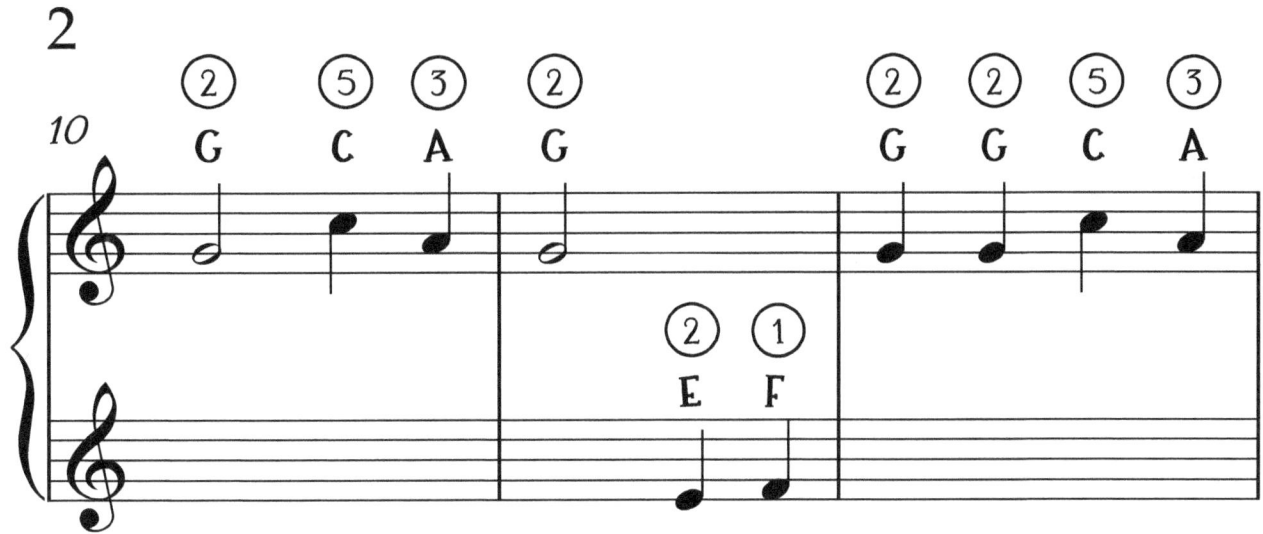
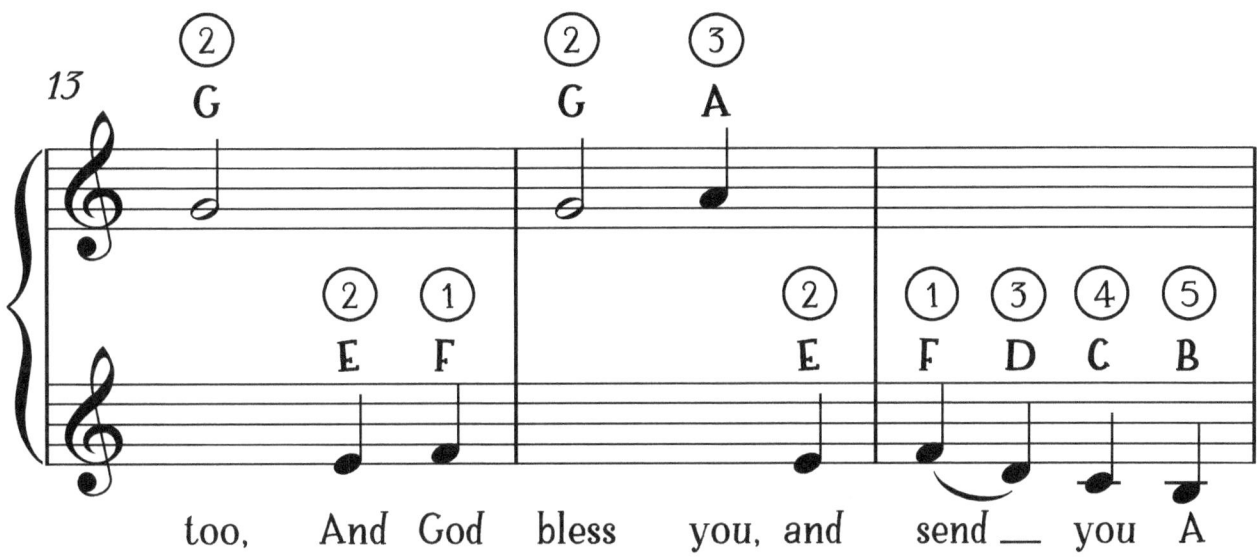
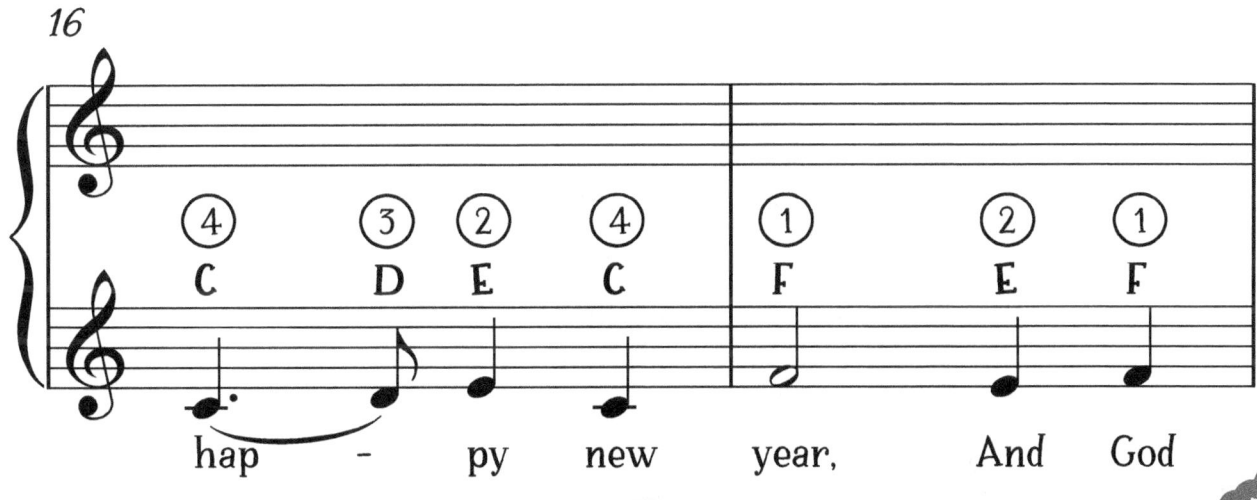

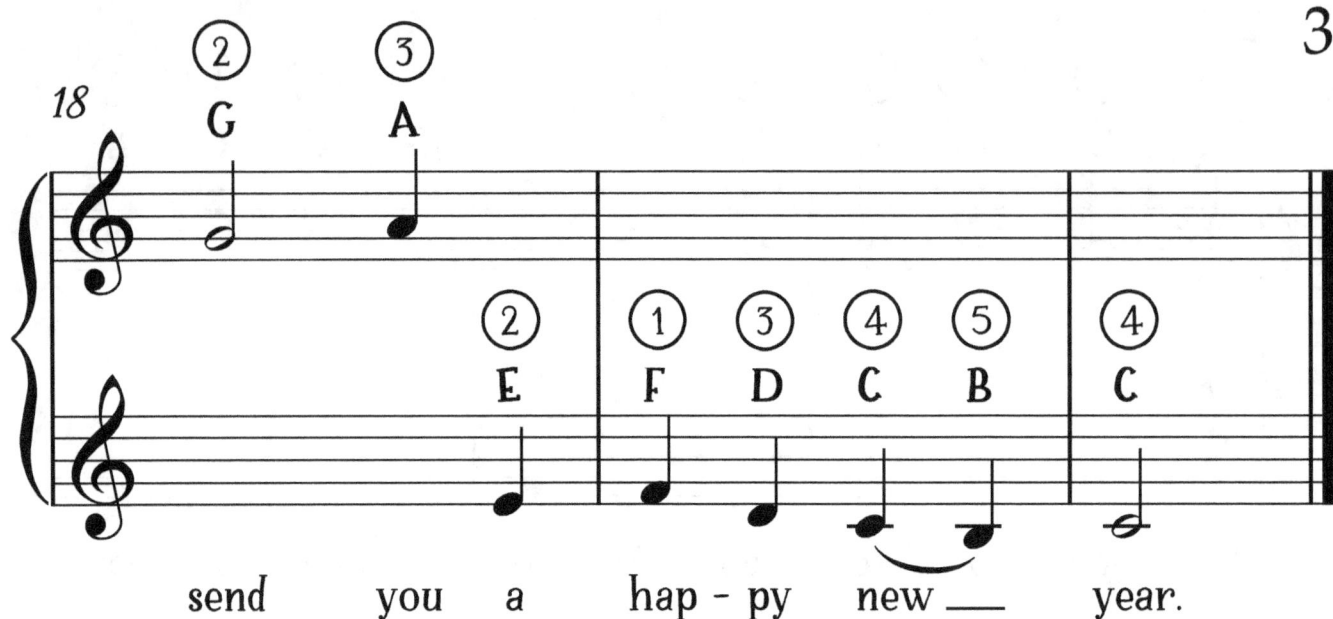

2. We are not daily beggars
   That beg from door to door,
   But we are neighbors' children
   Whom you have seen before.

Refrain

3. Good Master and good Mistress,
   As you sit by the fire,
   Pray think of us poor children
   Who wander in the mire.

Refrain

4. We have a little purse made
   Of ratching leather skin;
   We want some of your small change
   To line it well within.

Refrain

5. Bring us out a table,
   And spread it with a cloth;
   Bring us a moldy cheese and
   Some of your Christmas loaf.

Refrain

6. God bless the master of this house,
   Likewise the mistress, too;
   And all the little children
   That round the table go.

Refrain

USEFUL TIP

Watch out for accidentals in this song. You should play that sharp or flat for only one measure. After that, you will play the notes normally. Sometimes, time signatures can change as well. It looks like this in this song:

Refrain

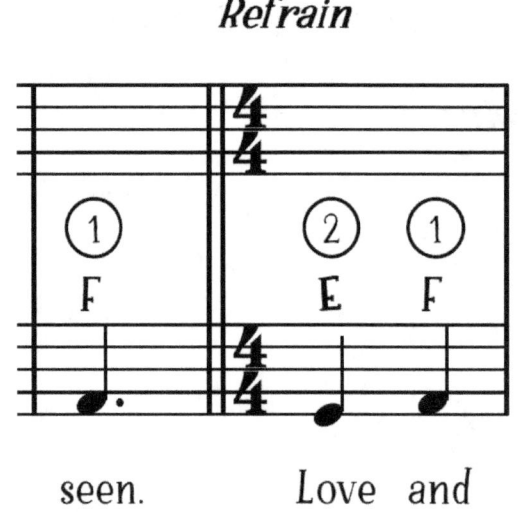

seen.   Love and

This means that from this bar you need to count in 4/4 instead of 6/8. It is not as difficult as it may seem. Just remember that this song is in 6/8 for the verses and 4/4 for the refrain.

The Twelve Days of Christmas

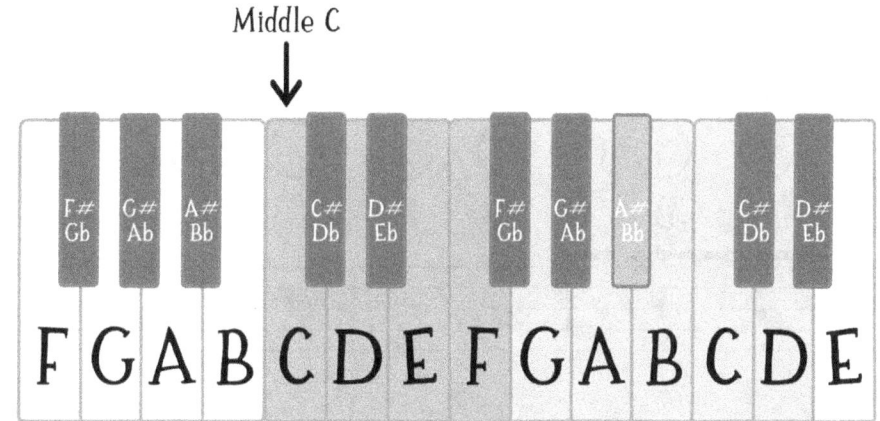

TWELVE DAYS OF CHRISTMAS

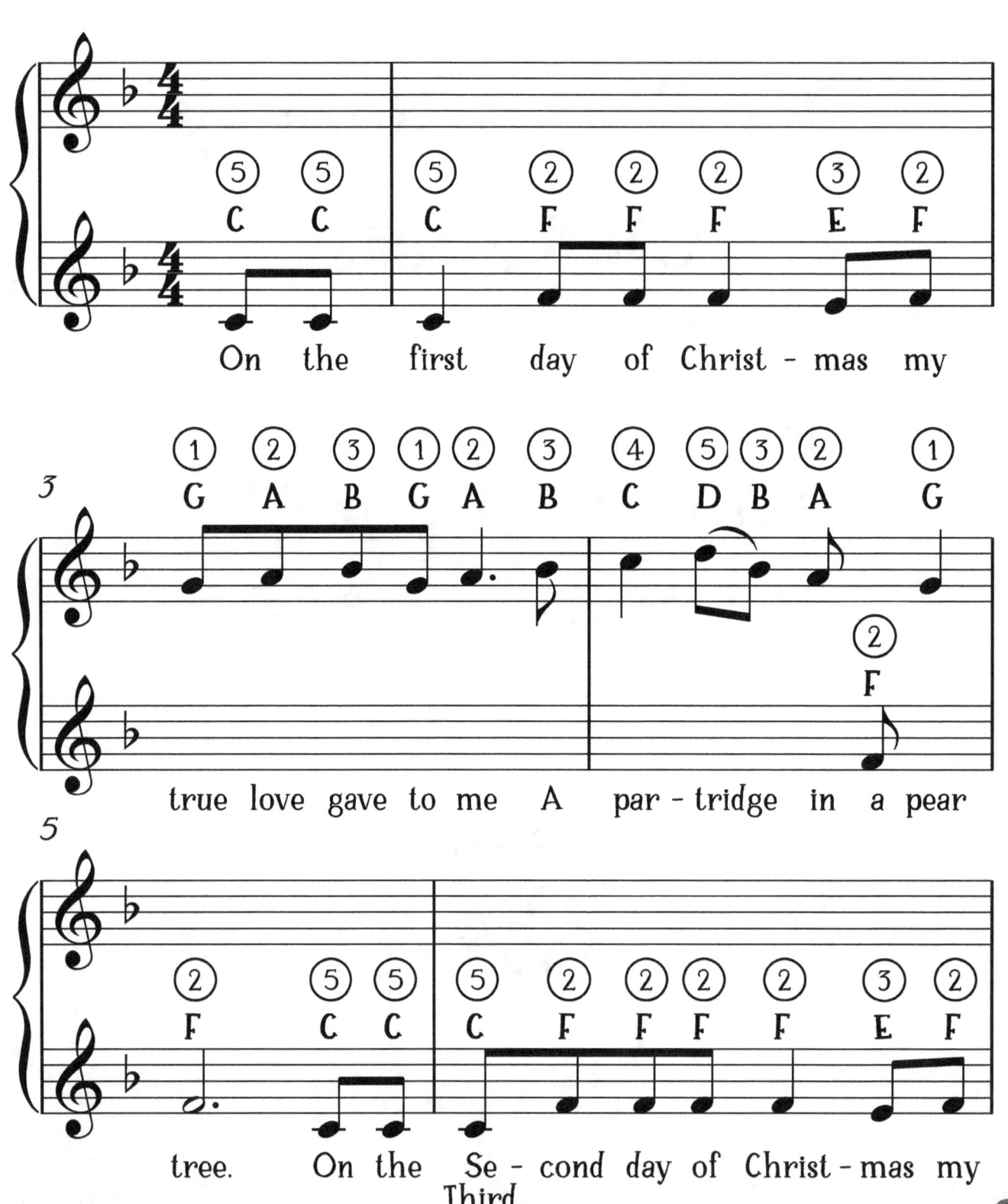

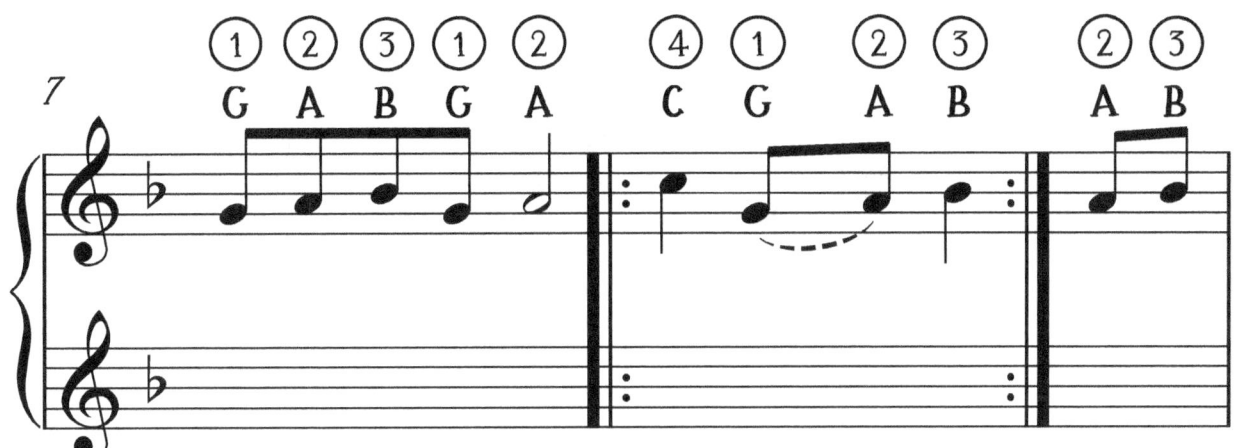

true love gave to me   Two tur - tle doves,   and a
                        Three french _ hens,
                        Four call - ing birds,

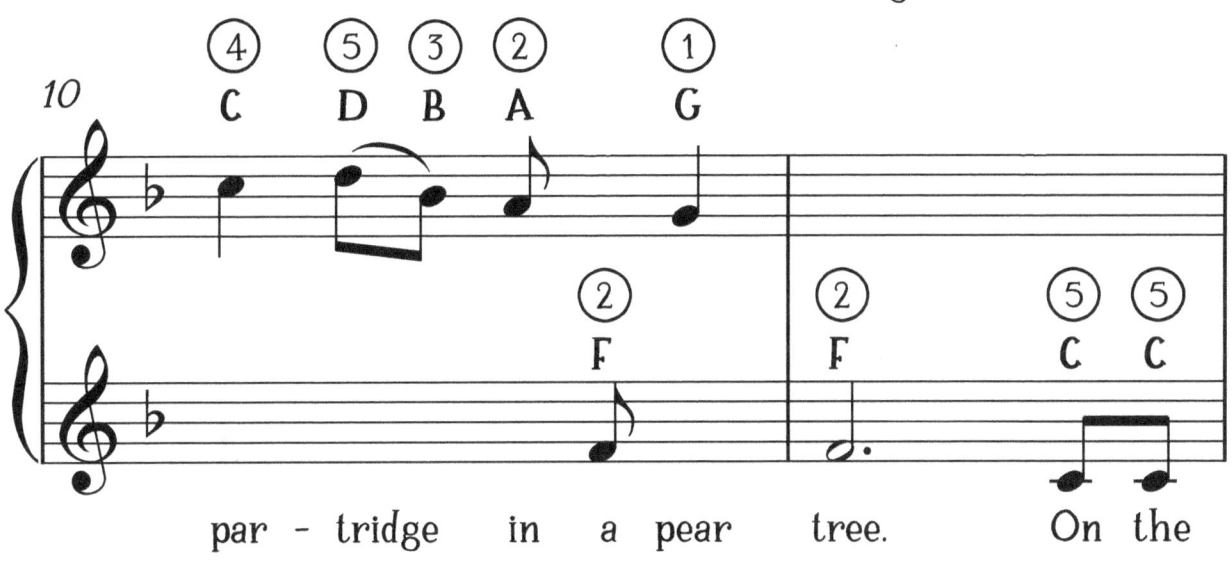

par - tridge   in   a   pear   tree.   On the

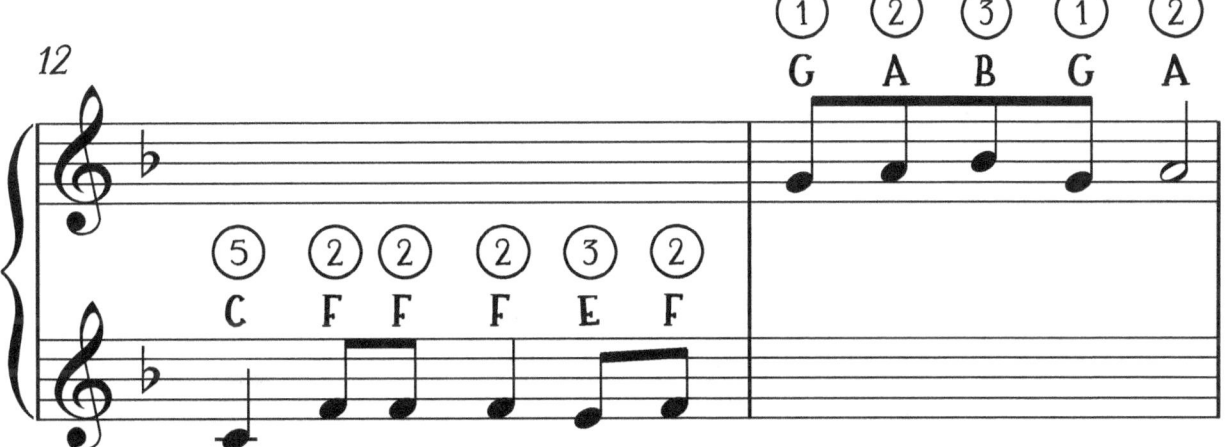

Fifth day of Christmas my   true love gave   to   me

14
4 5 3 4 4 3 2 1
C D B C C B A G
2
F
Five gold - en rings. Four _ call - ing birds,
17
3 1 2 3
B G A B
4 2 2 3 4 5
D F F E D C
Three french hens, Two ___ tur - tle doves and a
19
4 5 3 2 1
C D B A G
2 2 5 5
F F C C
par - tridge in a pear tree. On the

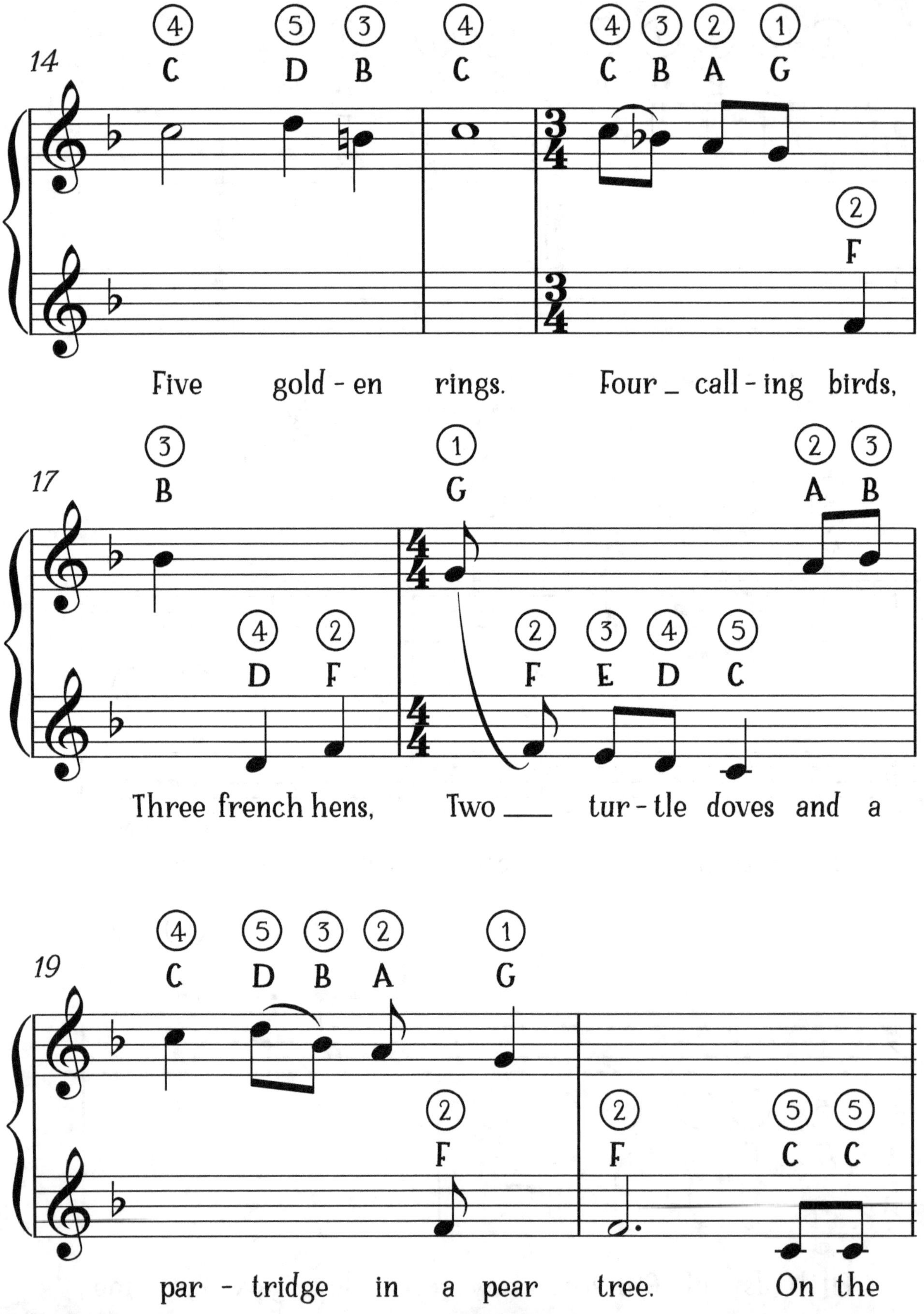

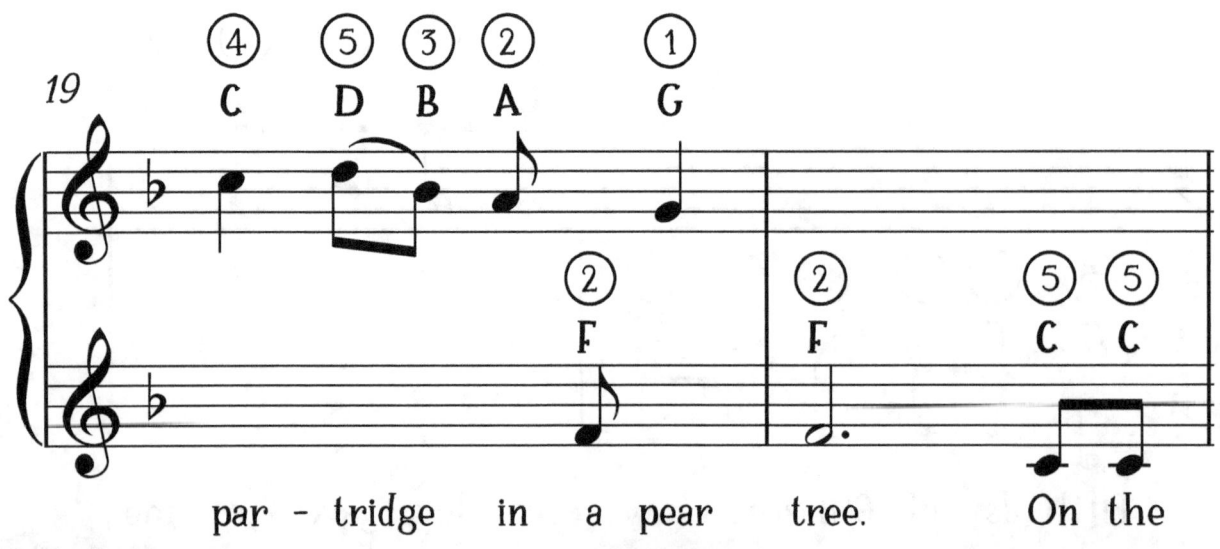

21

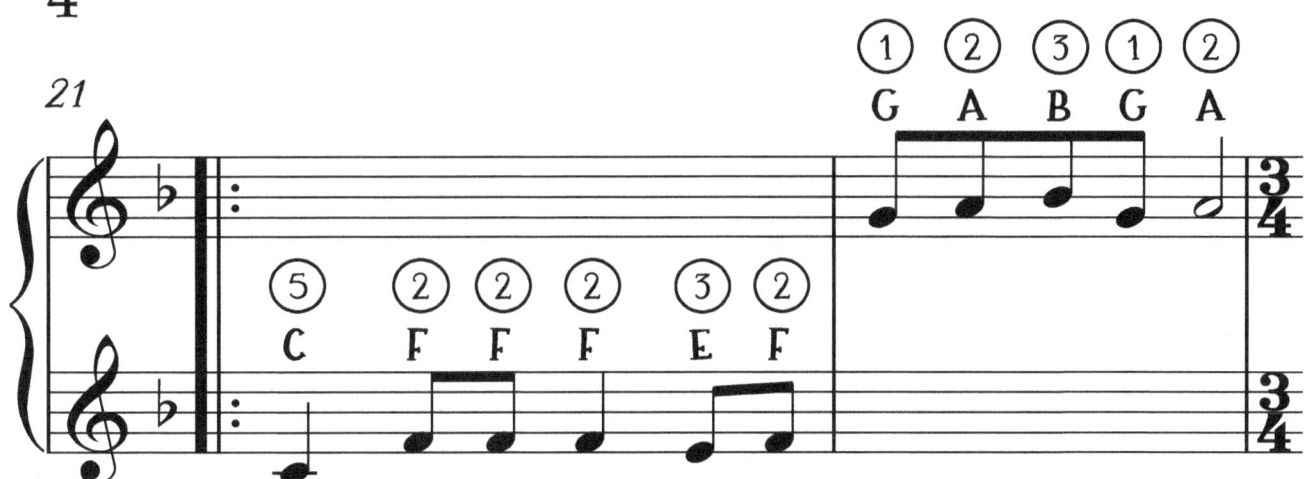

Sixth   day of Christ mas my true love gave to me
Seventh
Eighth
Ninth
Tenth
Eleventh
Twelfth

23

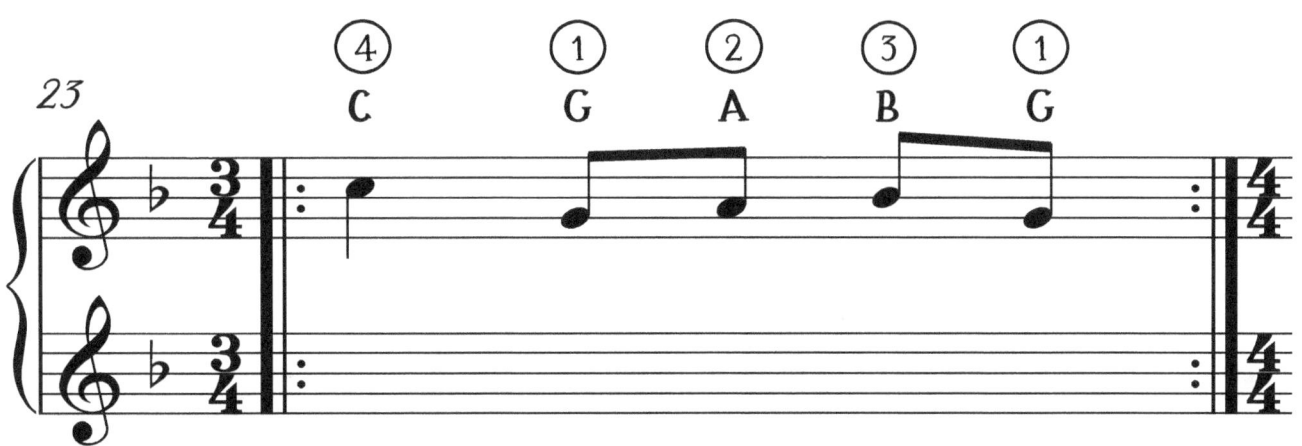

Six   geese   a - lay - ing
Seven   swans   a - swim - ing
Eight   maids   a - milk - ing
Nine   la - dies danc - ing
Ten   lords   a - leap - ing
Eleven   pip - ers   pip - ing
Twelve   drum - mers drum - ing

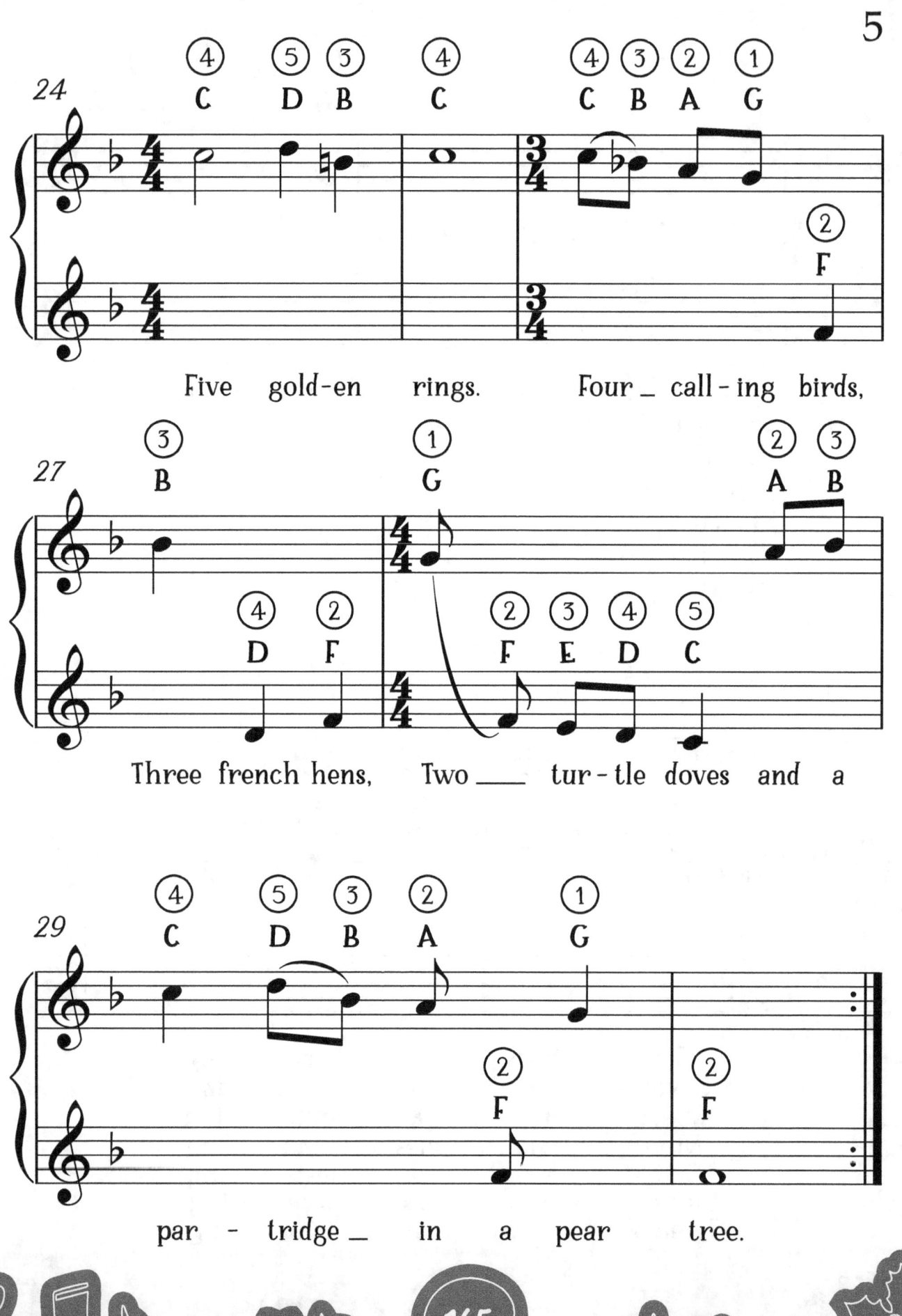

USEFUL TIP

In this song, time signature changes happen frequently. You will see changes from 4/4 to 3/4 and back many times-so watch closely! This is an em dash, longer dash.

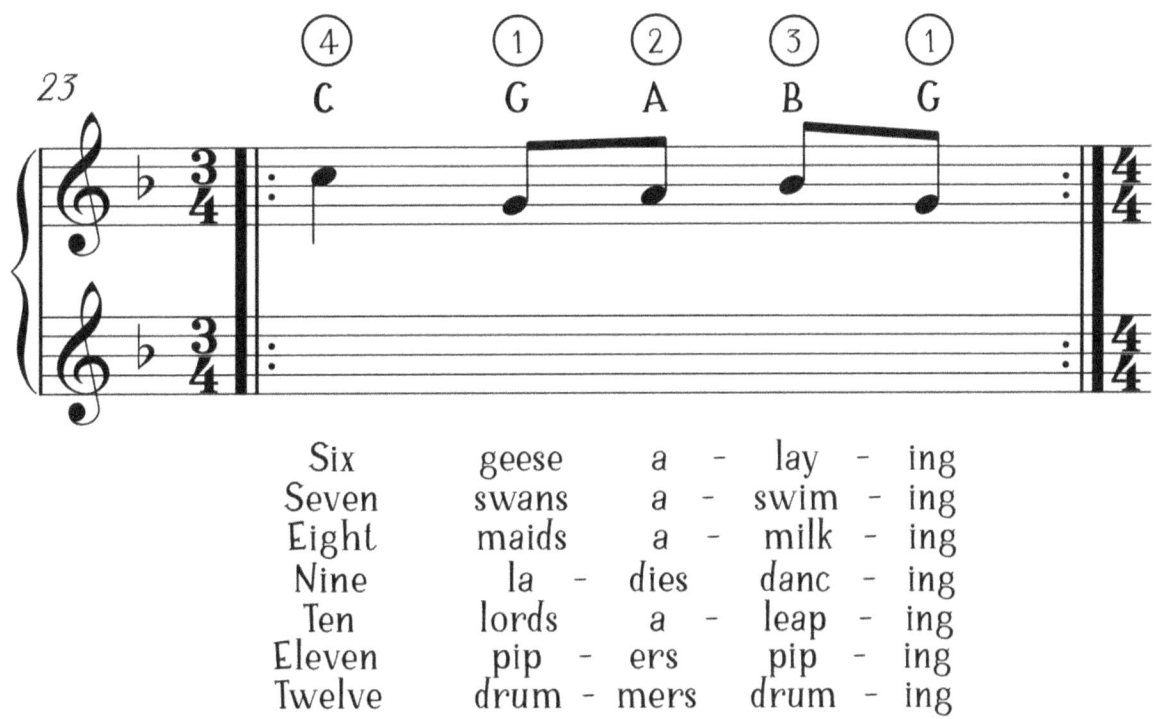

Six	geese	a	-	lay	-	ing
Seven	swans	a	-	swim	-	ing
Eight	maids	a	-	milk	-	ing
Nine	la	-	dies	danc	-	ing
Ten	lords	a	-	leap	-	ing
Eleven	pip	-	ers	pip	-	ing
Twelve	drum	-	mers	drum	-	ing

See those funny bar lines with the dots? Those are repeat signs. They tell us to repeat some part of the song with no changes. When you see this sign in place of the usual bar lines, you need to repeat this fragment. In this song, it doesn't mean you need to play it from the very beginning. Just the part that is between these two repeat signs-but this song is special, because you'll need to play this phrase seven times to list all the gifts!

Happy Christmas

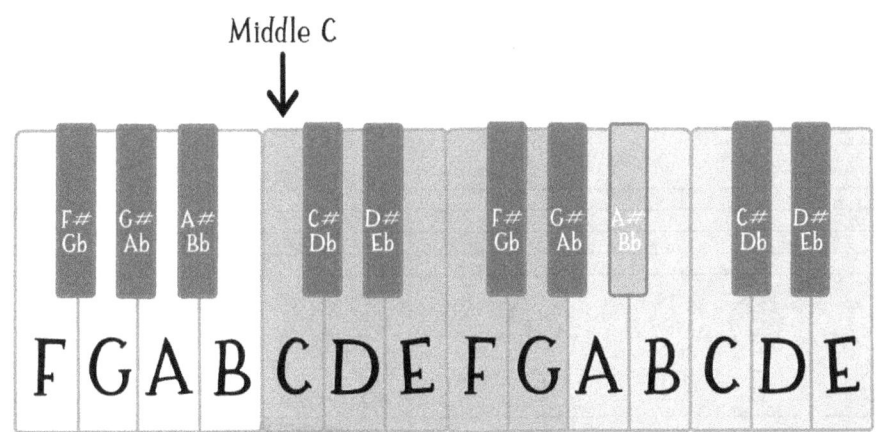

HAPPY CHRISTMAS

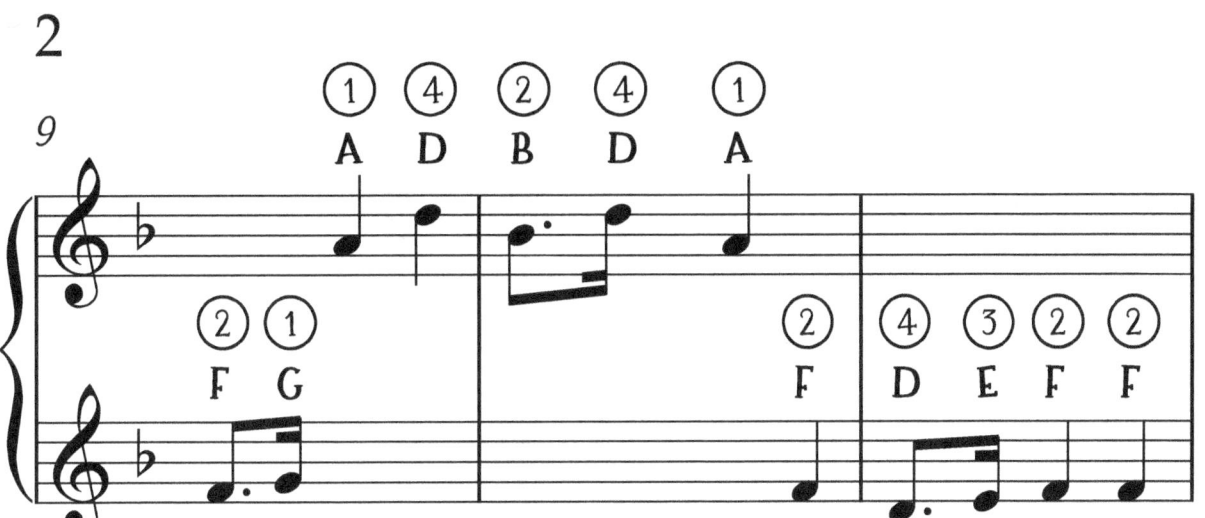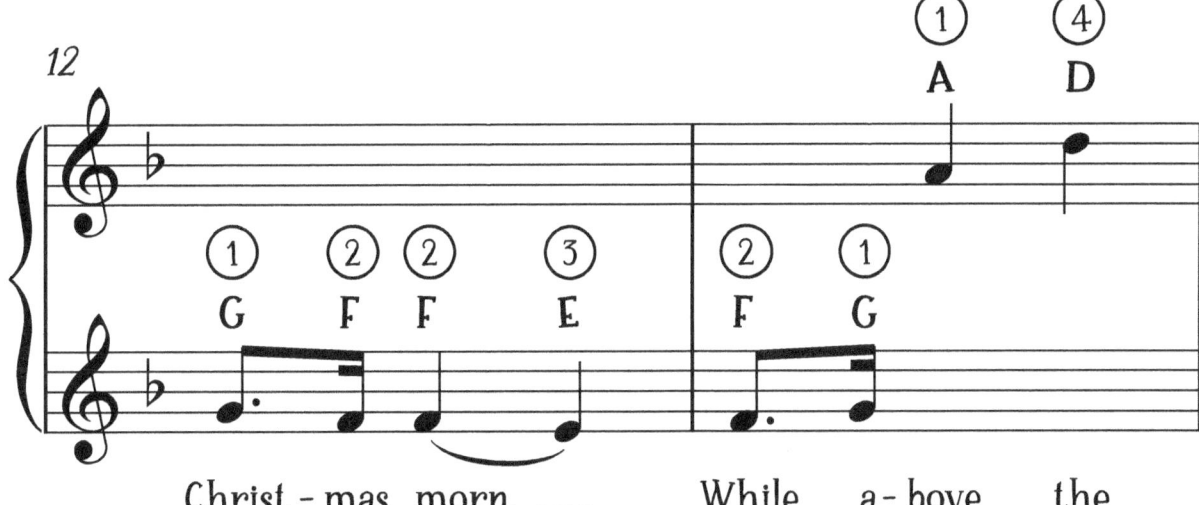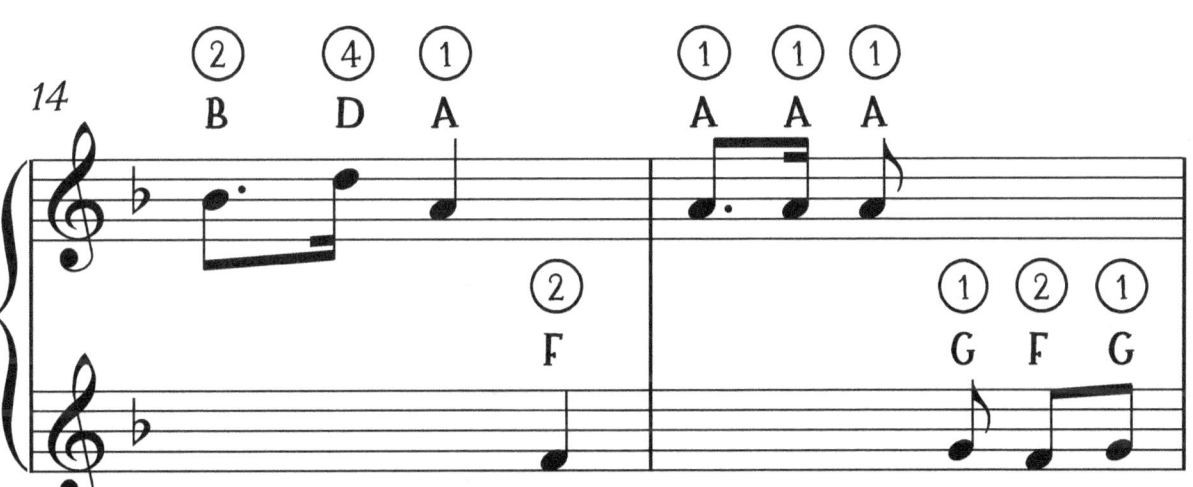

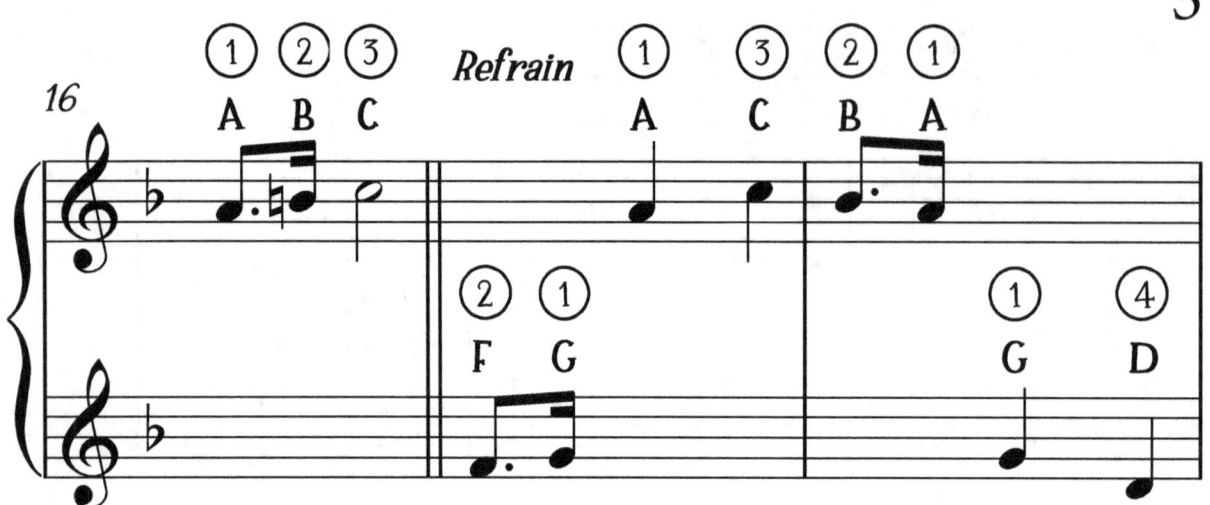
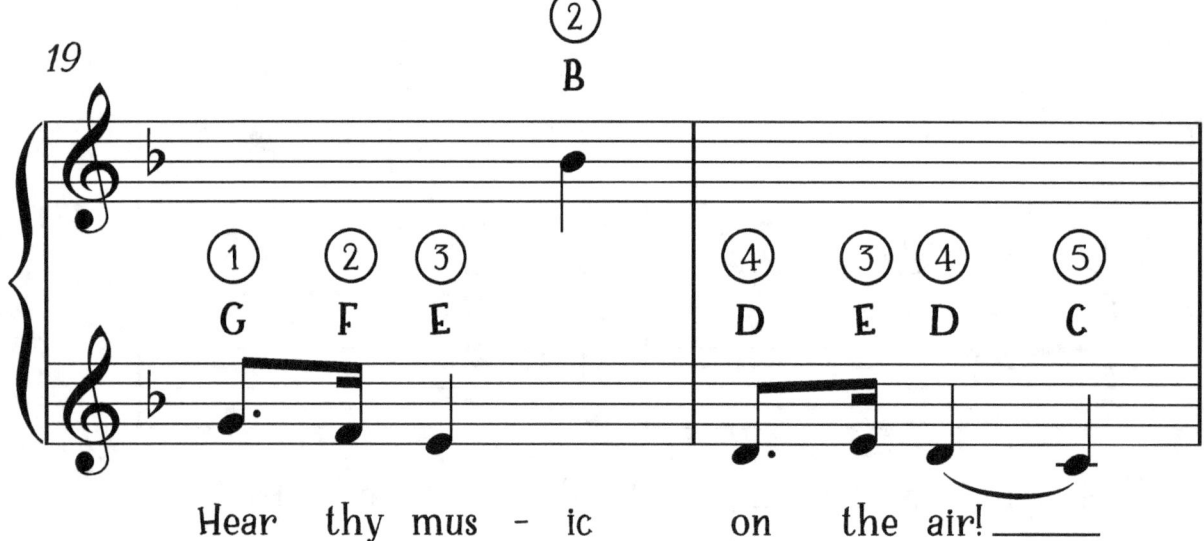
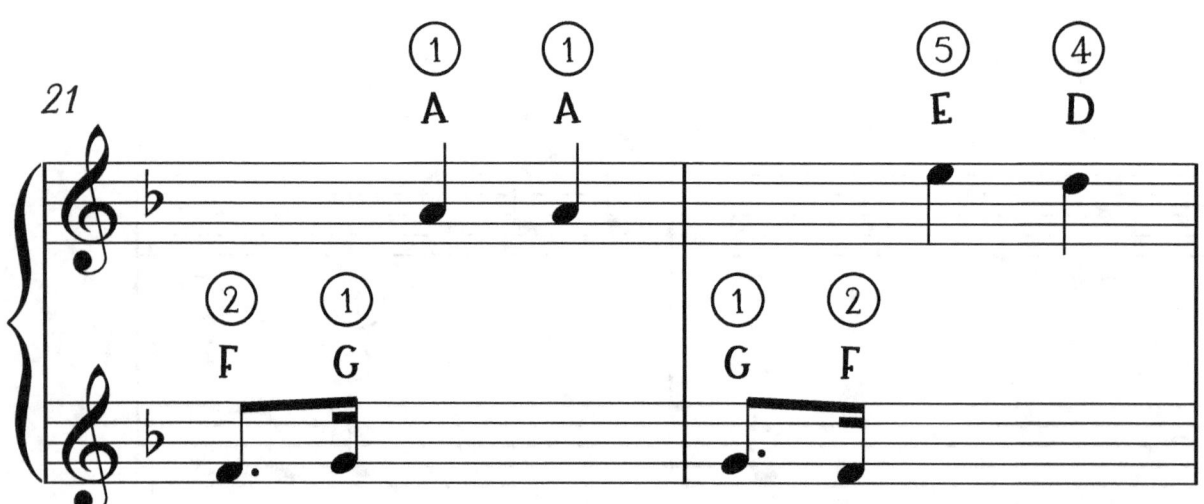

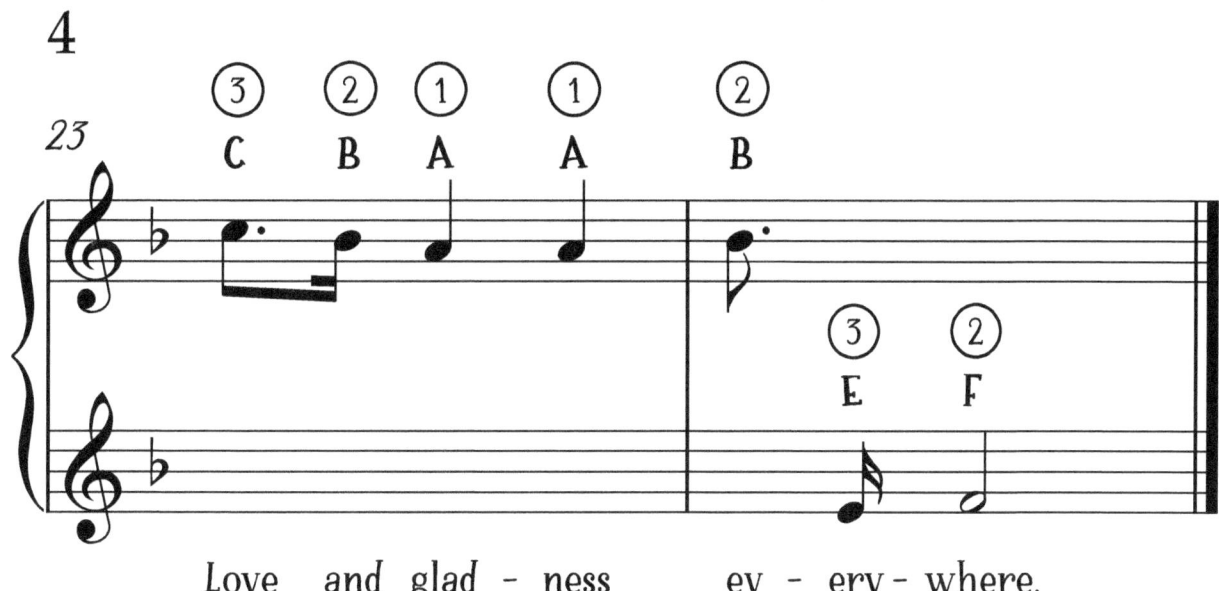

Love and glad - ness ev - er - y - where.

2. Not alone in far Judea,
   Under Bethl'em's starlit skies;
   In our hearts and homes the Christ-child
   Born anew, in beauty lies.
   Angel songs and pious raptures
   Humble folk and kings of earth,
   Joyous tidings, holy visions,
   Greet once more, Messiah's hallowed birth.

Refrain

3. Born anew in hearts made tender,
   Born anew in hearts made glad;
   To foretell the reign of goodness,
   And the downfall of the bad.
   Truth shall triumph over falsehood,
   Right be victor over wrong;
   Christian hearts! believe, proclaim it!
   Chant it in your grateful Christmas song!

Refrain

153

Go Tell It on the Mountain

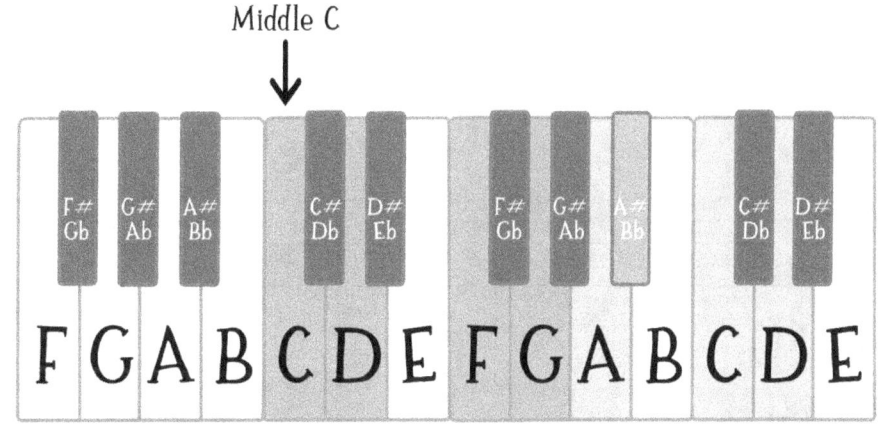

USEFUL TIP at the end of the song

GO TELL IT ON THE MOUNTAIN

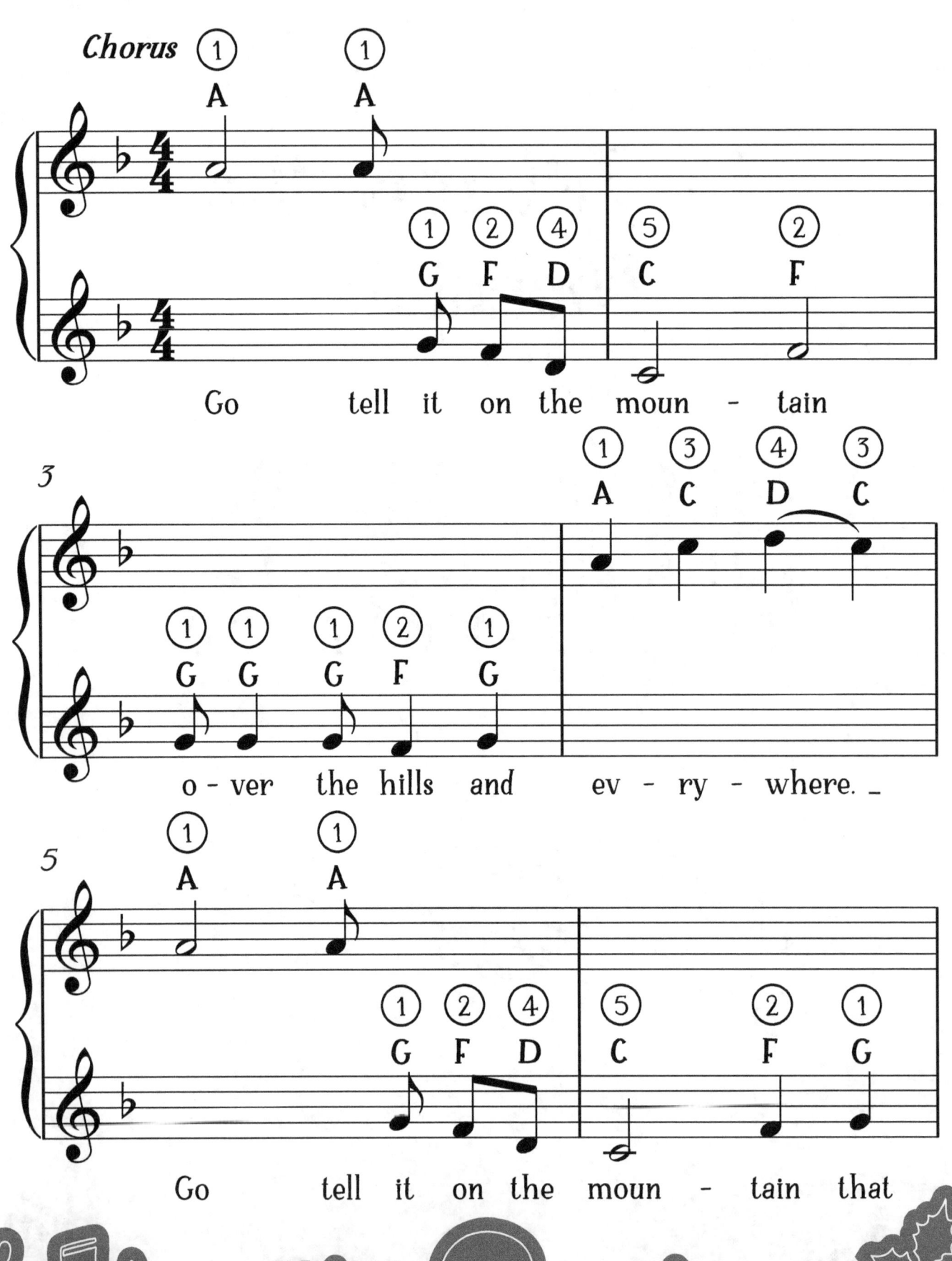

2. The shepherds feared and trembled
   When lo, above the earth
   Rang out the angel chorus
   That hailed our Savior's birth.

Chorus

3. Down in a lowly manger
   The humble Christ was born,
   And God sent us salvation
   That blessed Christmas morn.

Chorus

This song will be fun to play because it has some exciting rhythms. If you feel up to it, try playing this song with a swing. This means that instead of playing eighth notes evenly, you play them in a long-short, long-short pattern, almost like a dotted eighth note rhythm. You can imagine that your fingers are galloping. It gives the song a jazzy feel.

Syncopation

You will also meet a new type of rhythm. You can see it in this measure:

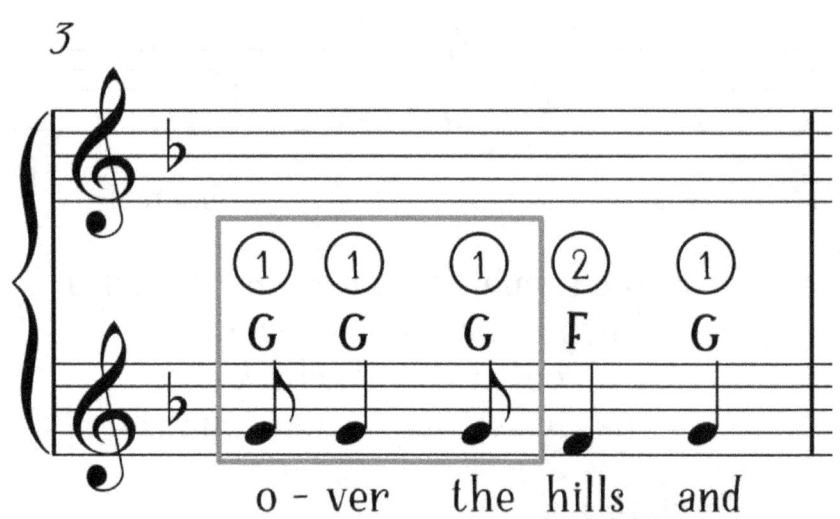

Instead of having the eighth notes together there is a quarter note in between. It creates a very particular sound. As if the accent is moved from its usual place on beat 2 to the "and" of beat 1. This can make it pretty challenging to play, since you want the accents to fall neatly on the beats. But this is also what makes this song so catchy! You just need to practice the rhythm before you play the song.

You can do it with a similar exercise as you had for dotted rhythm.

It Came Upon the Midnight Clear

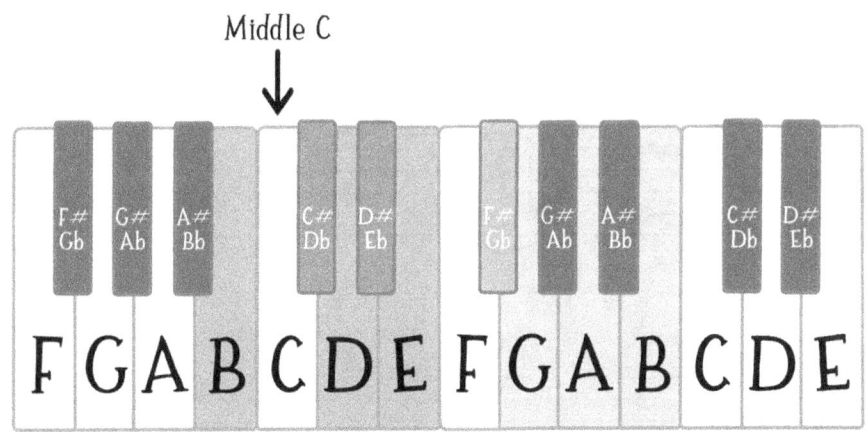

IT CAME UPON THE MIDNIGHT CLEAR

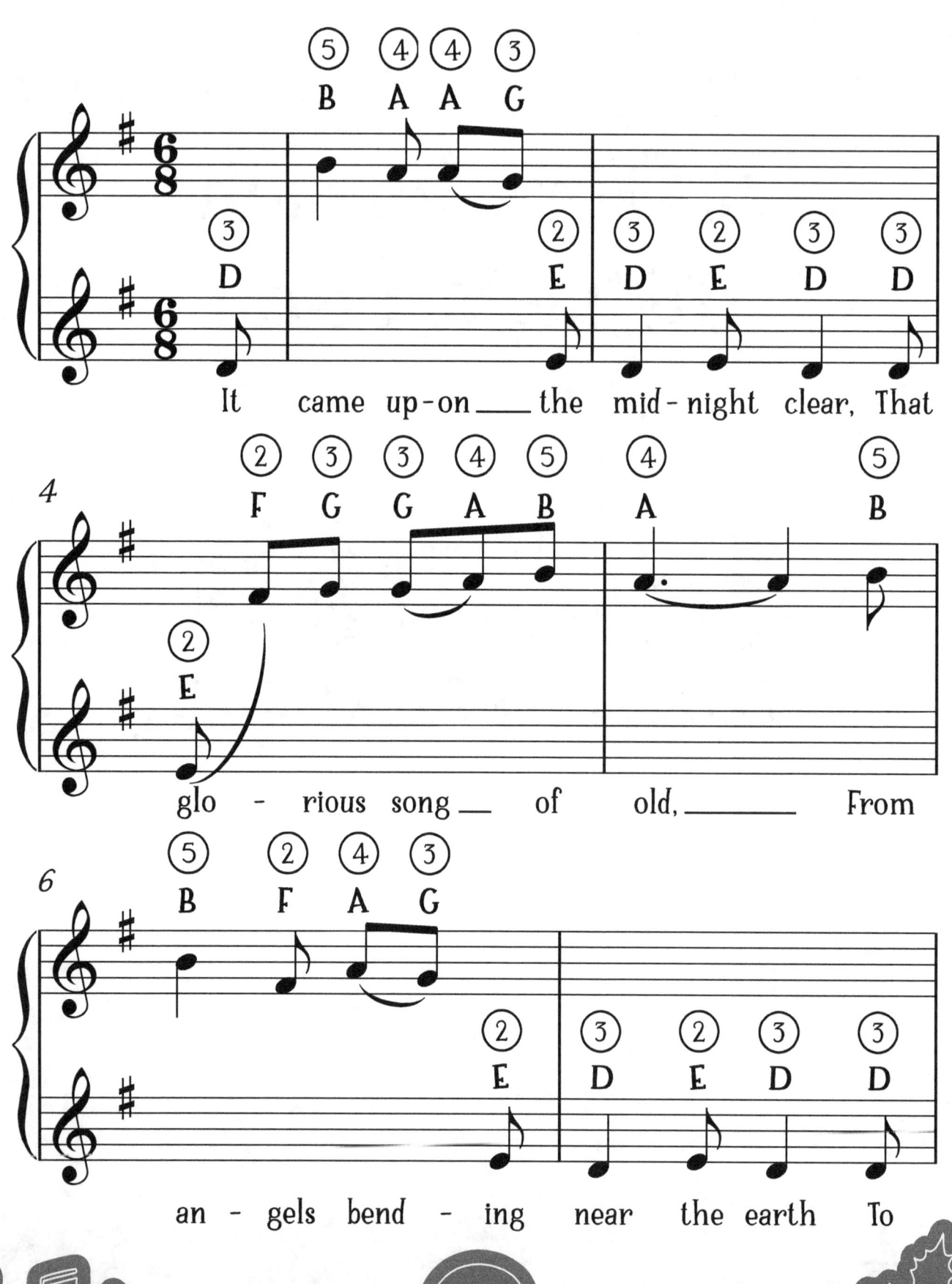

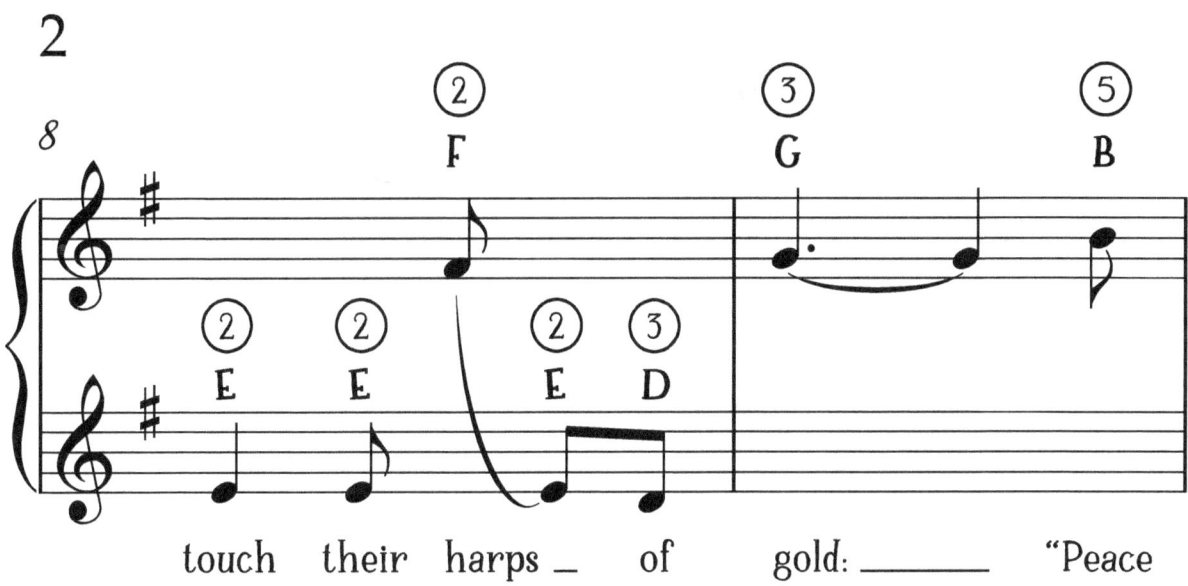
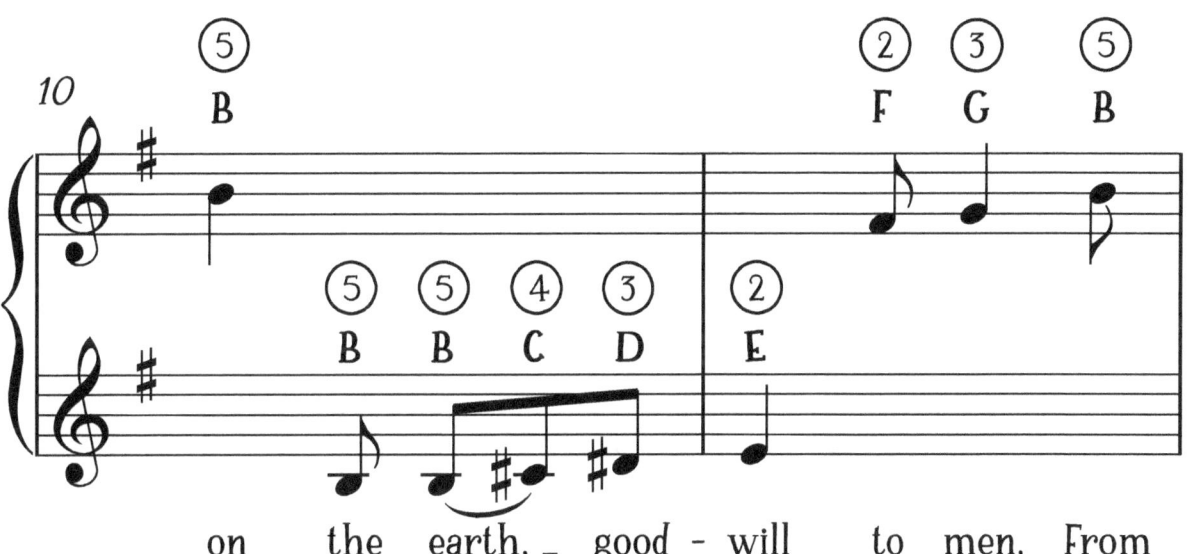
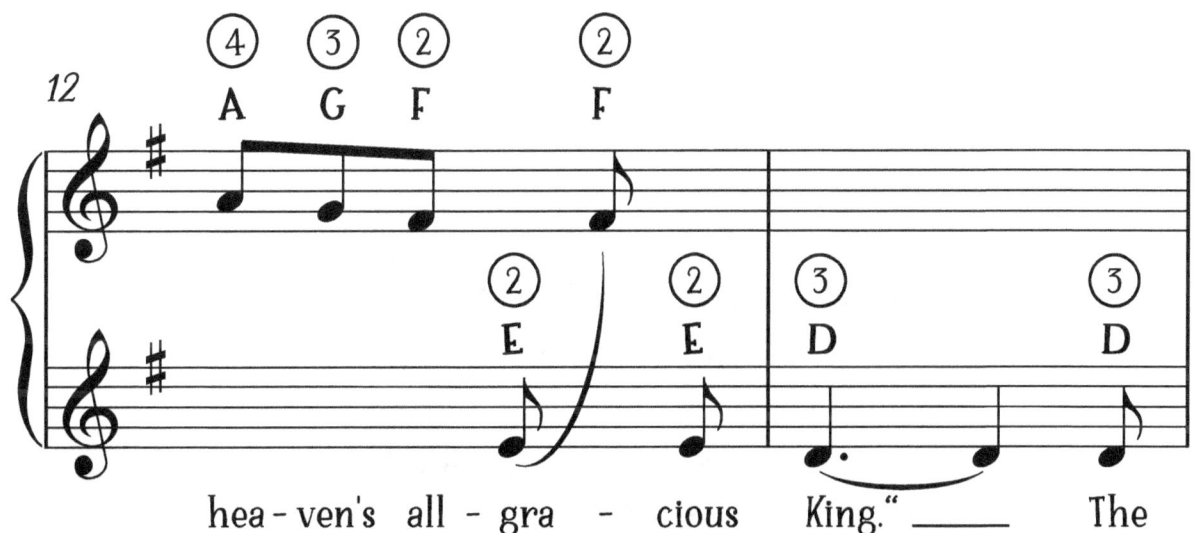

2. Still through the cloven skies they come
With peaceful wings unfurled,
And still their heavenly music floats
O'er all the weary world;
Above its sad and lowly plains,
They bend on hovering wing,
And ever o'er its Babel sounds
The blessed angels sing.

3. And ye, beneath life's crushing load,
   Whose forms are bending low,
   Who toil along the climbing way
   With painful steps and slow,
   Look now! for glad and golden hours
   Come swiftly on the wing.
   O rest beside the weary road,
   And hear the angels sing!

4. For lo! the days are hastening on,
   By prophet seen of old,
   When with the ever-circling years
   Shall come the time foretold
   When peace shall over all the earth
   Its ancient splendors fling,
   And the whole world send back the song
   Which now the angels sing.

Joy to the World

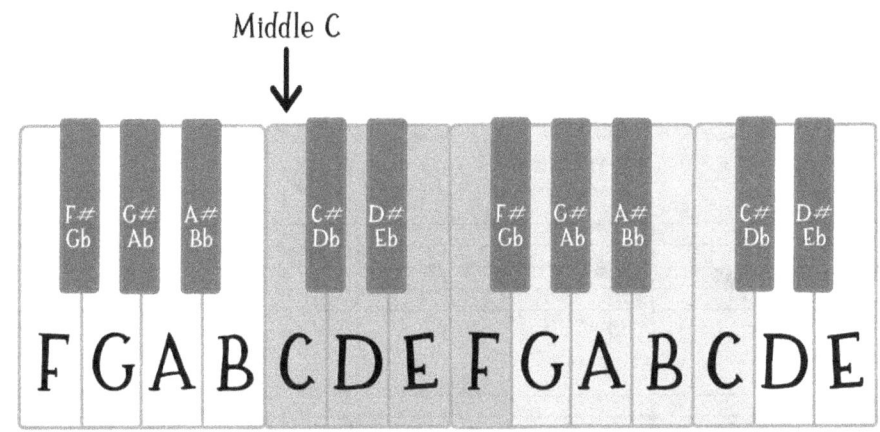

USEFUL TIP at the end of the song

JOY TO THE WORLD

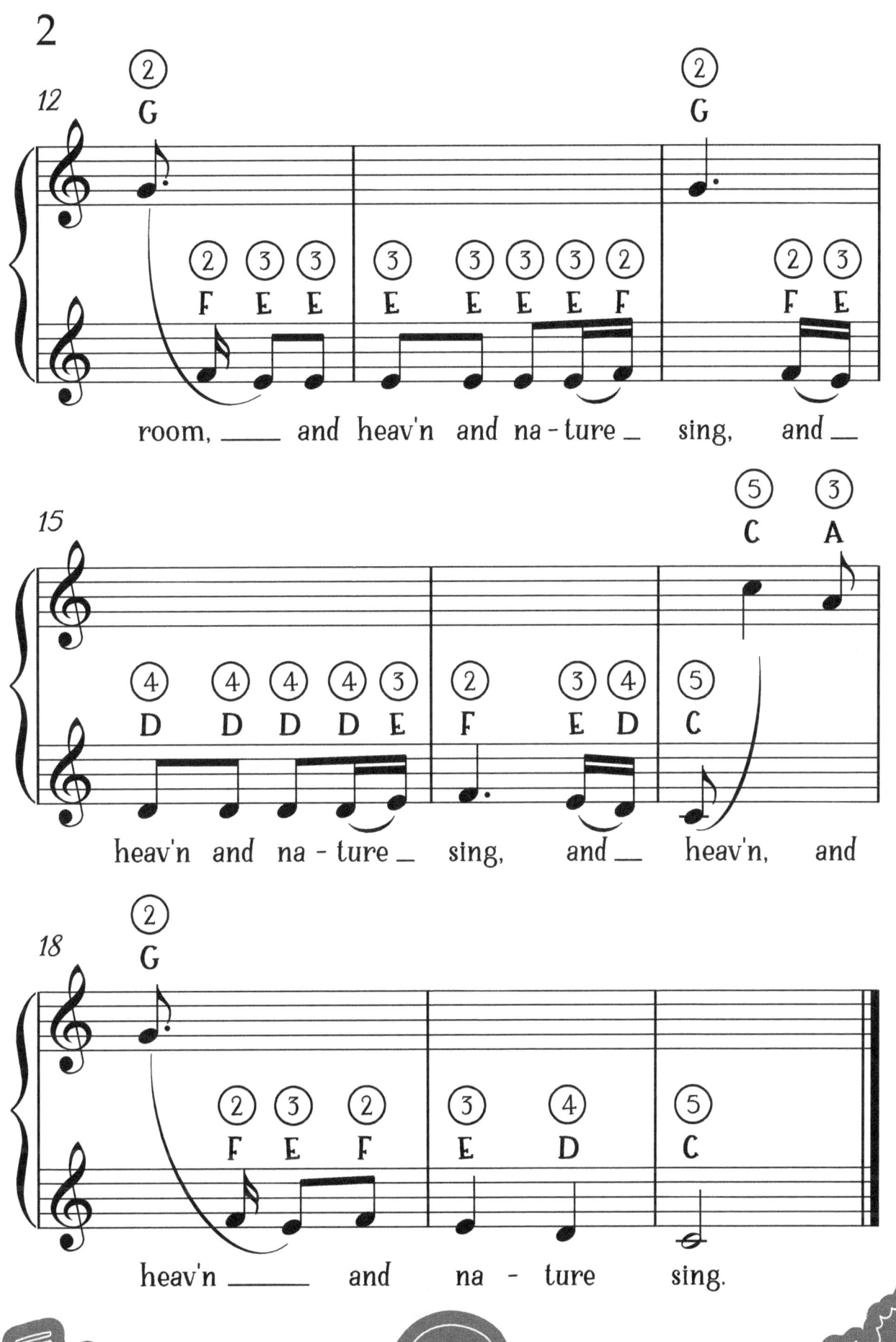

2. Joy to the earth, the Savior reigns!
   Let men their songs employ,
   While fields and floods, rocks, hills, and plains
   Repeat the sounding joy,
   Repeat the sounding joy,
   Repeat, repeat the sounding joy.

3. No more let sins and sorrows grow,
   Nor thorns infest the ground;
   He comes to make His blessings flow
   Far as the curse is found,
   Far as the curse is found,
   Far as, far as the curse is found.

4. He rules the world with truth and grace,
   And makes the nations prove
   The glories of His righteousness
   And wonders of His love,
   And wonders of His love,
   And wonders, wonders of His love.

In this song you can see one more type of dotted rhythm.

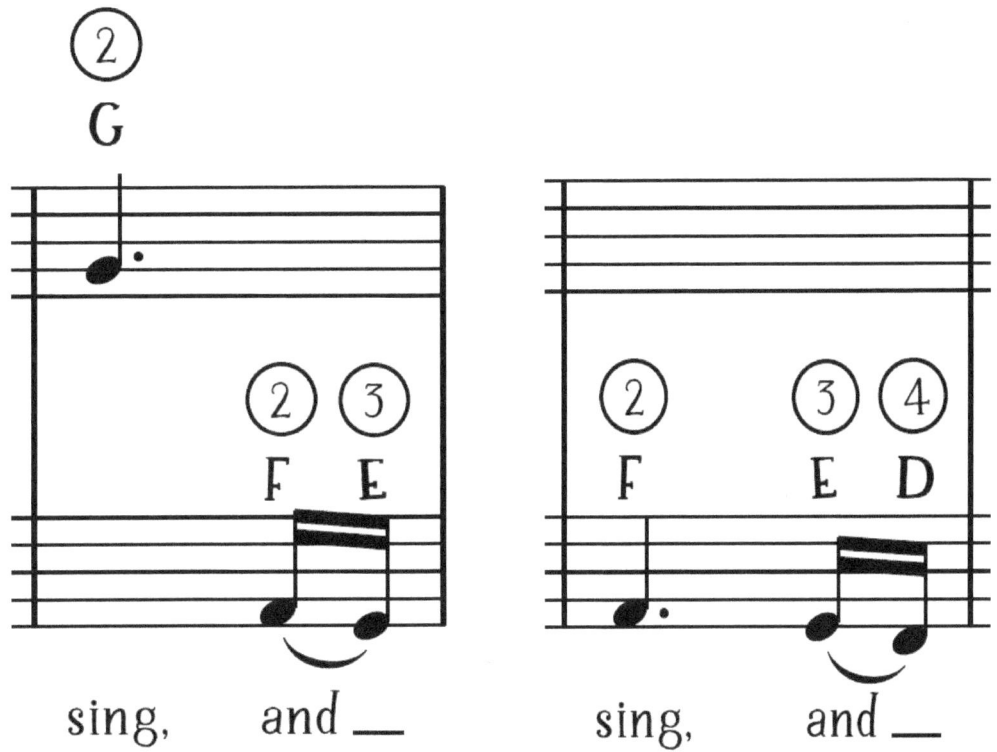

It works the same as a dotted quarter note with an eighth note. The only difference is that instead of an eighth note we have two sixteenths.

What Child Is This

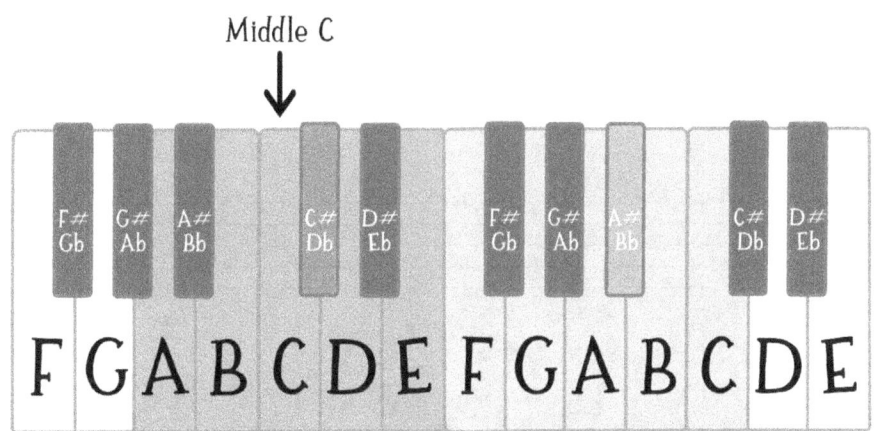

48. WHAT CHILD IS THIS?

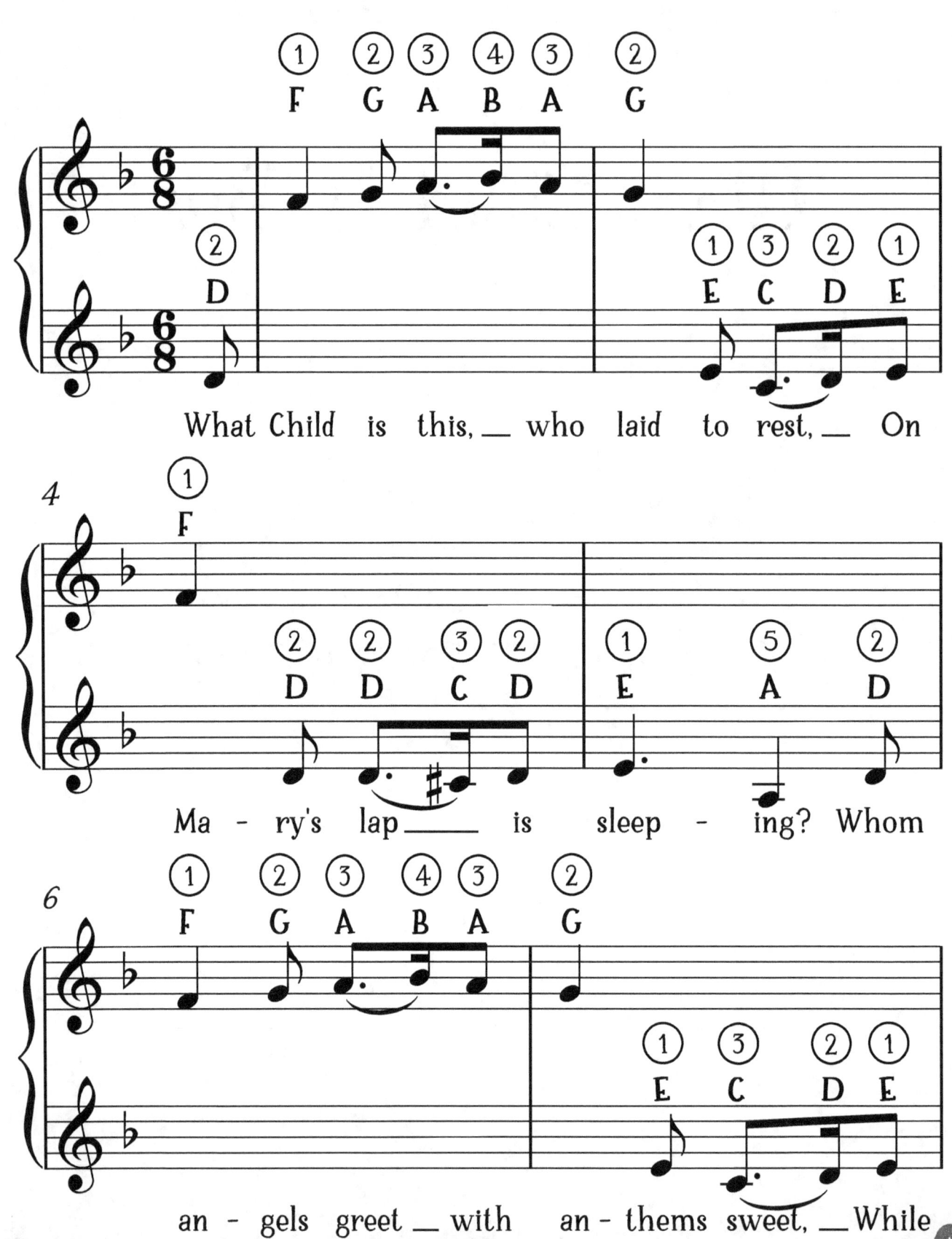

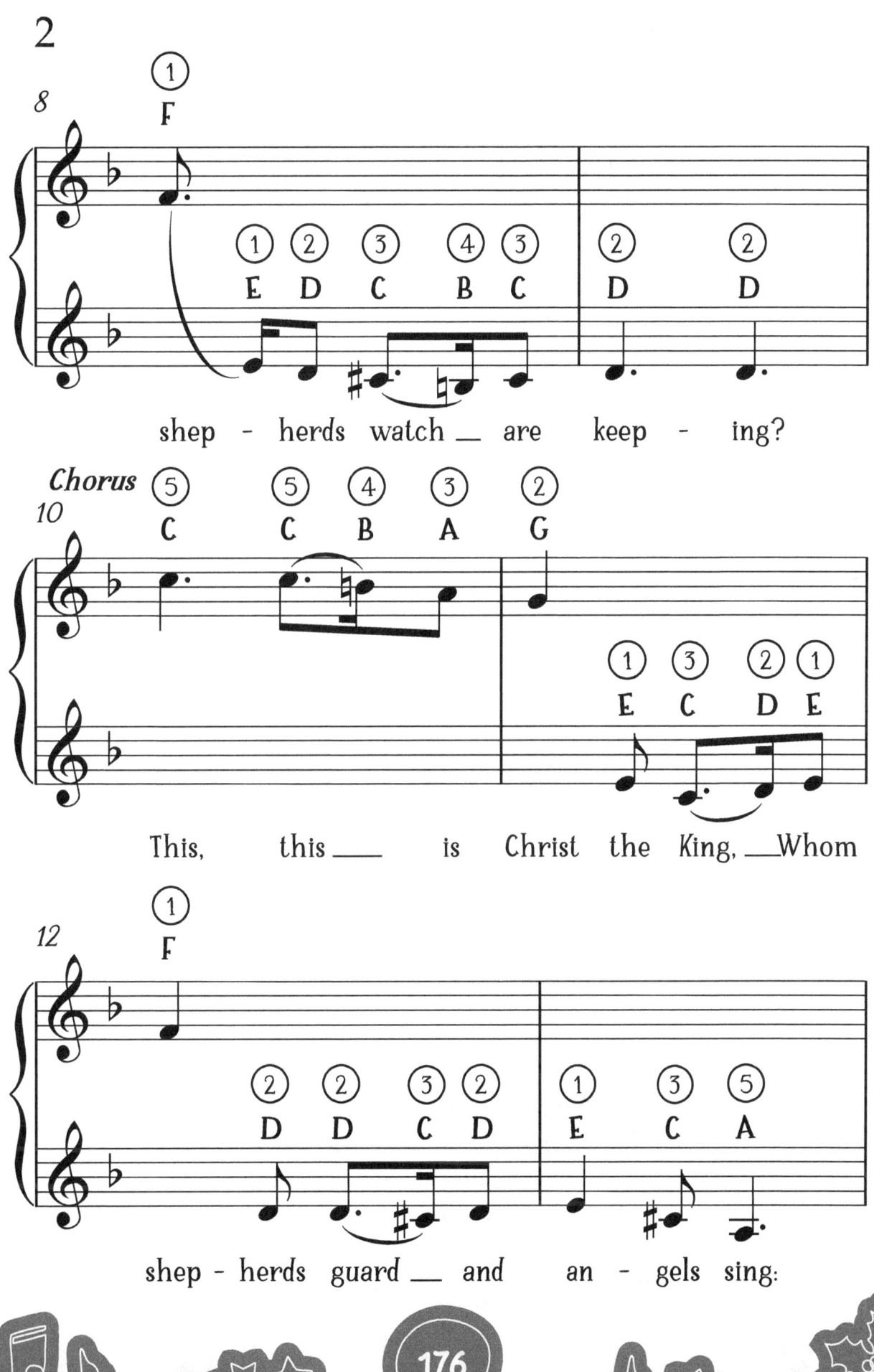

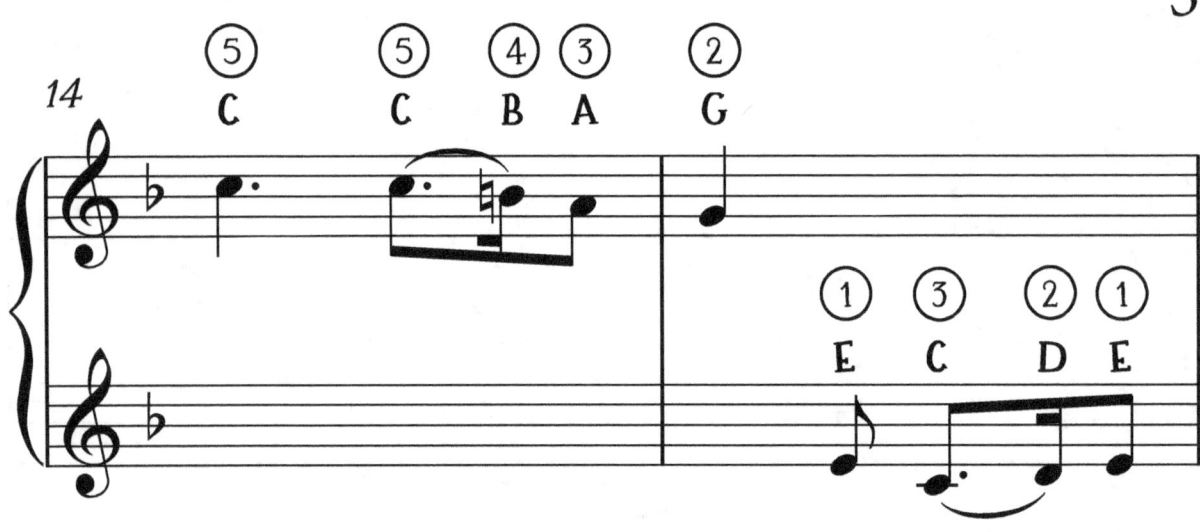

Haste, haste, to bring Him laud, The

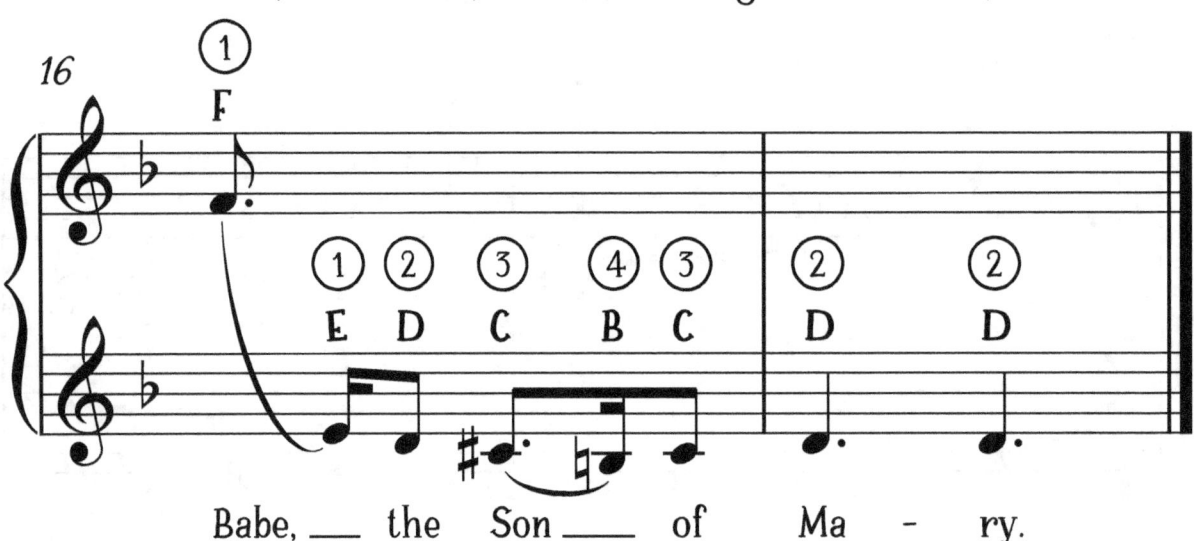

Babe, the Son of Ma - ry.

2. Why lies He in such mean estate,
   Where ox and ass are feeding?
   Good Christian, fear: for sinners here
   The silent Word is pleading.

Chorus

3. So bring Him incense, gold, and myrrh,
   Come, peasant, king to own Him.
   The King of kings salvation brings;
   Let loving hearts enthrone Him.

Chorus

Oh, Holy Night

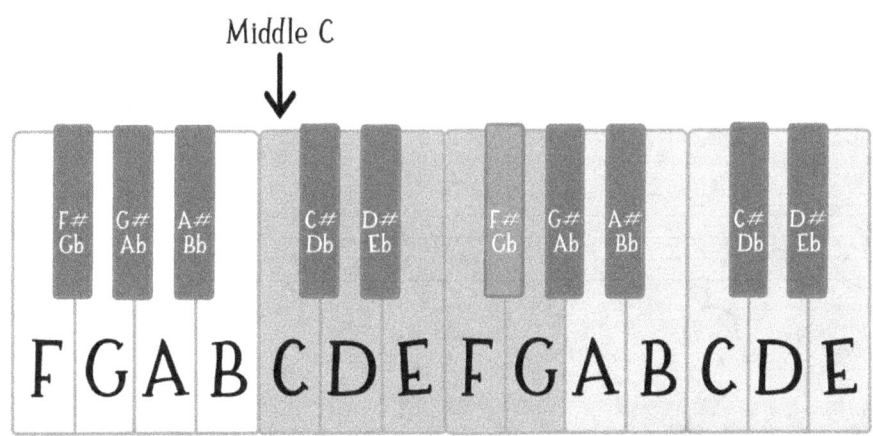

OH, HOLY NIGHT

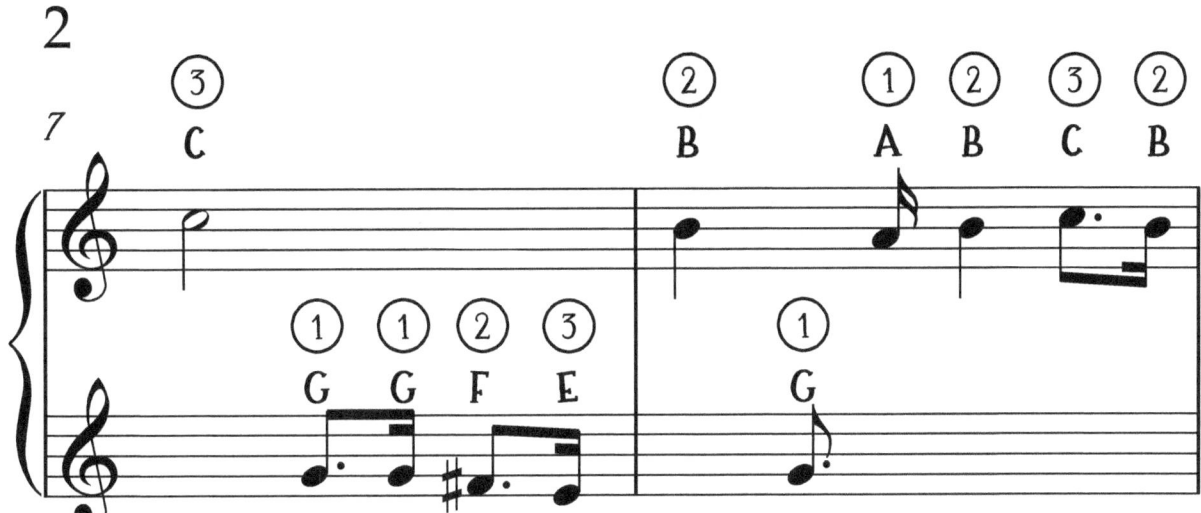

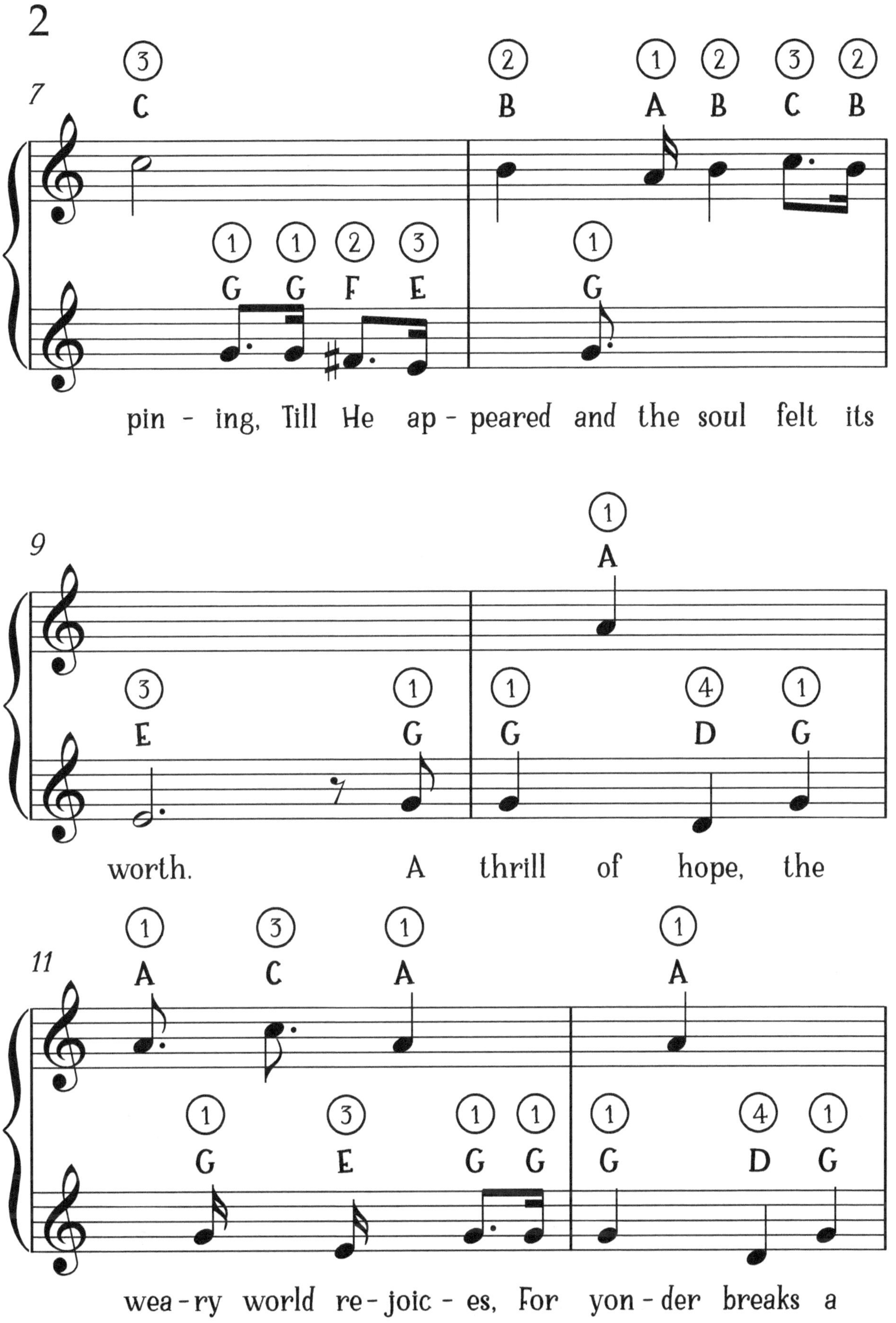
2
7
C B A B C B
G G F E G
pin - ing, Till He ap - peared and the soul felt its
9
A
E G G D G
worth. A thrill of hope, the
11
A C A A
G E G G G D G
wea - ry world re - joic - es, For yon - der breaks a

night   di - vine,   oh, night,   oh, night di - vine!

2. Led by the light of faith serenely beaming,
   With glowing hearts by His cradle we stand.
   So led by light of a star sweetly gleaming,
   Here came the Wise Men from Orient land.
   The King of kings lay thus in lowly manger,
   In all our trials born to be our Friend.
   He knows our need— to our weakness is no stranger.
   Behold your King, before Him lowly bend!
   Behold your King, before Him lowly bend!

3. Truly He taught us to love one another;
   His law is love and His gospel is peace.
   Chains shall He break, for the slave is our brother,
   And in His name all oppression shall cease.
   Sweet hymns of joy in grateful chorus raise we;
   Let all within us praise His holy name.
   Christ is the Lord! O praise His name forever!
   His pow'r and glory evermore proclaim!
   His pow'r and glory evermore proclaim!

Conclusion

As we wrap up this festive musical journey, I want to thank you for your hard work and enthusiasm in exploring the magical world of piano music. I've loved guiding you through these joyful songs, from classics like "We Wish You a Merry Christmas" and "Silent Night" to cheerful tunes like "Jingle Bells" and "Up on the House Top." Along the way, you've discovered how sharps, flats, dotted rhythms, repeat signs, and even syncopation can make music exciting and fun. As you close this book, remember that your music adventure is just beginning-like a never-ending holiday celebration! Keep discovering new songs, experimenting with rhythms, and enjoying every moment of making music. Just as the holiday season is filled with joy and wonder, let your practice be bright and cheerful. Keep playing with a big smile, and let your musical journey shine all year long!

Happy playing!

night   di - vine,   oh, night,   oh, night di - vine!

2. Led by the light of faith serenely beaming,
   With glowing hearts by His cradle we stand.
   So led by light of a star sweetly gleaming,
   Here came the Wise Men from Orient land.
   The King of kings lay thus in lowly manger,
   In all our trials born to be our Friend.
   He knows our need— to our weakness is no stranger.
   Behold your King, before Him lowly bend!
   Behold your King, before Him lowly bend!

3. Truly He taught us to love one another;
   His law is love and His gospel is peace.
   Chains shall He break, for the slave is our brother,
   And in His name all oppression shall cease.
   Sweet hymns of joy in grateful chorus raise we;
   Let all within us praise His holy name.
   Christ is the Lord! O praise His name forever!
   His pow'r and glory evermore proclaim!
   His pow'r and glory evermore proclaim!

Conclusion

As we wrap up this festive musical journey, I want to thank you for your hard work and enthusiasm in exploring the magical world of piano music. I've loved guiding you through these joyful songs, from classics like "We Wish You a Merry Christmas" and "Silent Night" to cheerful tunes like "Jingle Bells" and "Up on the House Top." Along the way, you've discovered how sharps, flats, dotted rhythms, repeat signs, and even syncopation can make music exciting and fun. As you close this book, remember that your music adventure is just beginning-like a never-ending holiday celebration! Keep discovering new songs, experimenting with rhythms, and enjoying every moment of making music. Just as the holiday season is filled with joy and wonder, let your practice be bright and cheerful. Keep playing with a big smile, and let your musical journey shine all year long!

Happy playing!

www.ingramcontent.com/pod-product-compliance
Lightning Source LLC
Chambersburg PA
CBHW081617100526
44590CB00021B/3477